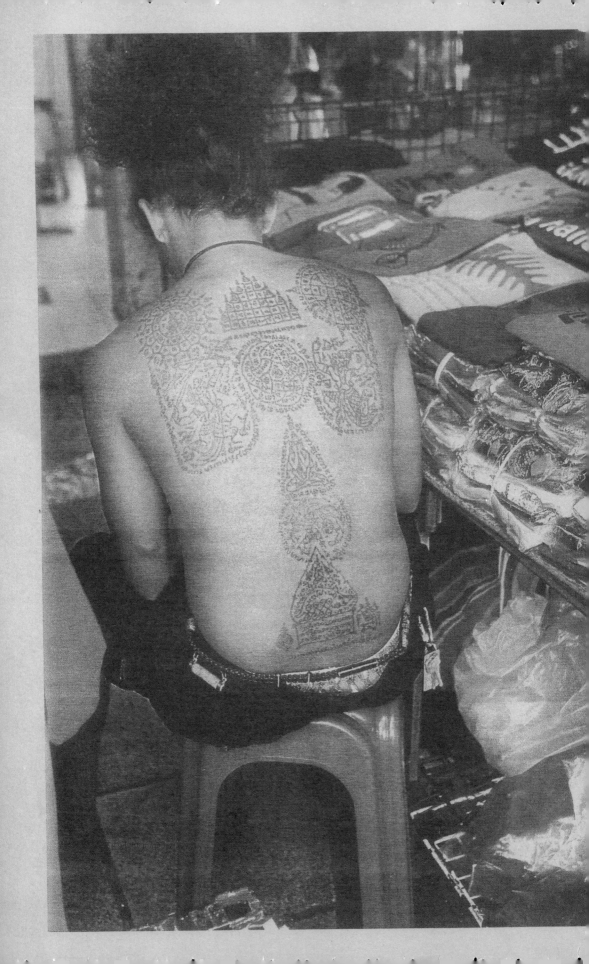

Raw:
Pervasive Creativity in Asia

To Richard,

May there be
pervasive creativity
in our business!

Kind regards,

Kunal.

For Sumona, Sukanya and Shourya, Jane,
Chloe, Scarlet and Charlie

Kunal Sinha + David Mayo

Raw

Pervasive Creativity in Asia

Photographs by Steffen Billhardt + Thomas Billhardt + Kunal Sinha

Published in the UK in 2012 by
Clearview Books
11 Grosvenor Crescent
London SW1X 7EE

A CIP catalogue record for this book is
available from the British Library

ISBN 1 908337 12 2

Printed in the Far East

Introduction

In the commercial world, we 'manufacture' creativity. We decide what we want to sell, to whom and then we conjure the environment and the most engaging way of delivering that message. We use a left brain process to deliver right brain outputs. And the success rate is falling! Consumers, in contrast, use creativity in response to situations: in their relationships, to solve problems, in order to stand out or define their identity. In today's digital world, their success rate is rising because they have more tools and options at their disposal and because of this their sources of inspiration are more than ever.

THE EMOTIONAL CONNECTION

As we have learned more about the capabilities and the inner workings of the human brain, the single most important ingredient in staying ahead is the emotional connection between a brand and its consumer. To do this, science proves that it is the right side of the brain – or the creative side – that needs to be deployed if we are to connect more intimately and meaningfully. However, this is not just true of commercial creativity, it is true of any company operating in a world where employees and consumers are – by definition – one step ahead of the boardroom. The boardroom is a place where the left brain prevails and yet it is on the street where the right brain fights – and wins – everyday. Education develops our rational left brain. But if you look at the way humankind innovates, you see that, in contrast to how we are educated, we use several natural skills to build things from seemingly nothing. First among these skills is the application of the right brain, and the catalyst seems to rest with one thing and one thing alone – creativity.

MY CONSUMER DOESN'T UNDERSTAND

This book was born of a repetitive experience; confronted with new creative ideas on brief and designed to take a client's product, service or brand to the stars, the brand manager would often baulk and respond by professing that "this is too creative for my consumer!" We were – admittedly instinctively – quite sure they would understand the work. This stock response was at once designed to make sure that advertising agencies didn't further their own creative agenda by winning awards on work for clients that was either irrelevant or ineffective. But it was also designed to close the synapse between the agency and the client. With the closure of that synapse goes the creative leap of faith that separates the ordinary from the outstanding. But we've found that a similar attitude towards consumers prevails beyond the marketing function within companies: managers are generally thought to be better judges of innovation than their customers. The creative synapse, once closed, does not allow for the bravery and creativity required to penetrate deeply into a consumer psyche. Advertising creativity considered on its own for its own sake will always fail in research – be that the brand manager's agenda or the researcher's LINK test, focus group or neuro-testing.

THE CASE FOR CREATIVITY - EMOTION SELLS

We believe that for creativity to be truly considered, it has to be considered in only two ways: retrospectively and in its own environment. And by one group of people – the people that it was intended for. All the research, insights, cultural knowledge and personal experience count for less (even when added together) than the consumer response.

We know that emotion sells. In fact, in advertising, people as far back as the great Albert D. Lasker in the 1940s were telling us how a feeling is more powerful than hard rationale. In the 21st century, with advances in neuroscience, we can prove it. However, these are simply reducing the risk factor that will inevitably be played back by, to use a word, 'The Market'. There is no substitute for making a start.

As one sage boss once said; "Nothing will ever be achieved if all obstacles are to be overcome first." How true! We believe this to be even more timely in Asia, currently the world's economic powerhouse.

Raw: Pervasive Creativity in Asia is a book that shows just how creativity forces its way out of every crevice in every environment around Asia. For this to be relevant in today's environment where every advertising dollar is scrutinised for its return on investment, it is worth noting that most of what is in this book includes a sales angle. Sales are what allow us to earn a livelihood. If you don't sell, you don't earn. If you don't earn you don't survive. And so it is for brands.

STAND OUT OR BLEND IN

There are several ways in which brands can, do and will behave in this environment. Two are foremost among them: stand out or blend in. Brands and their communication can lead, follow or act as a catalyst, but for them to have any effect they must live and thrive in an environment. They have to have contact with a variety of other stimuli for them to activate and become potent rather than latent. Brand communications are combustible and incendiary. They have – by their very definition – to be so.

It is exactly the same in business. Look at any list of top ten business books and you will find several titles that refer to the notion of creativity in business. Creativity in business, according to Harvard Business Review, is not just about having ideas, rather it is about seeing them through and making them happen in a motivating, engaging and productive way. Managers who are prepared to push with the courage of their convictions and act in a way that they can neither explain nor sometimes define are the managers who will win.

IF IT WORKS - CARRY ON

Many of the people who are displaying their creativity in this book are people who do things rather than talk about doing things. They clearly show that creativity is essential to growing business. It is about taking a risk and trusting your gut, as many of the entrepreneur owners and the managers in some of Asia's most successful companies do. Many of them have succeeded in defining themselves through their brands and the work they allow their agencies to produce for them as Twin Peaks examples of where creativity has driven effectiveness. But for all the talk of creativity, on bookshelves, in offices, and reviews at business schools, *Raw* is founded deeply in reality. There are no 'office words', no processes, no group discussions and gloss on the street. It is a moving experiment which reveals what works and does not work. If it works, you keep doing it. If it doesn't work, then you stop and try something new.

Understanding how to develop commercial creative work for consumers can only be done by knowing consumers. Who they are, how they speak, by being amongst them. And even then, we can only really predict the outcome of our creativity by a small and invisible amount. That said, all the people in this book are real. Their creativity is natural. It hasn't been put there for any other reason than economic survival (we call that effectiveness in the office). They don't have awards shows, they don't have Executive Creative Directors and teams trying to 'crack a brief' and they certainly don't have people deciding what is and isn't good for them (or what they will and will not understand). There are no filters other than the response of The People on the Street. The laws of the market are the same laws that either allow creativity to do its job or force it to fail. The laws that the common consumer in his or her everyday life, rewrites each day with each new interaction and transaction.

CREATIVITY AS A CATALYST FOR GROWTH

We have presented this book in order to bring some of the chaos back into creativity. We believe that creativity can be a catalyst for growth. We respect the unknown almost as much as we deride caution. We want to re-focus the point of creativity back into a business context. We want to show how it works where the rubber meets the road and that no matter how much an agency sits and formularizes and presents and insists, there is no substitute for trying and proving it. For being there and seeing it stand or fall. And, of course, to make it stronger the next time around.

We live in a world where everything is the same. Where vanilla greases the progression of the careerist. Where caution keeps the wheels of commerce turning. There is no place for mistakes, which are generally frowned upon and chided. But this is changing. In a vanilla world, the ingredient that is missing from the boardroom is creativity. Ways in which to see the world in different ways. Ways of tackling problems in new and innovative ways. Changing behaviour in order to change an outcome. The essential, intangible ingredient in today's commercial world is creativity. Whether you are the manufacturers of creativity like advertising agencies, whether you are daring performers like Cirque de Soleil, or those in need of a different look at their business or specific business problem, the ability to use the right side of the brain is the part where the innovation lives and will differentiate you. Innovation is your competitive edge – just as it is in the bustle of the street.

Raw is designed to see creativity itself in a new and uncluttered way. You could almost say that we have taken a new and creative look at creativity. But if you bring everything back to commercial creativity and the role of the advertising agency in the new post-recession, digitised world, the new mediascape is allowing brands to do many things. But there seem to be four at the core:

1. Blend in, rather than stand out
2. Whisper, not shout
3. Interact, not command
4. Be iterative, rather than sequential

Agencies operating in this mediascape are changing to deliver in this world and be accountable for the investment made on behalf of their clients. This in turn is changing the way they are being remunerated. And the marketers themselves now have more choices than ever before; of media channels, creative approaches and agencies. But one area where there is less choice is finding the impresarios and entrepreneurs inside the full service agencies to deliver these plans – those senior enough to cut through and 'hands-on' enough to deliver powerfully and effectively.

Asian consumers are more demanding, discerning and dismissive than ever before, and it is the collaborative and the iterative that will prevail. This is as much a record of what they have achieved through their creativity, as a tribute to their native, raw ingenuity. In today's world, they have the answers. We can learn from them, and serve as mediators and interlocutors. The only thing impeding success in this environment is the way the marketers, their partners and their agencies are set up to set the ideas of common people free.

David Mayo

Contents

Are Asians creative?

Salman Khan, not to be confused with the eponymous Bollywood star, runs the world's most popular educational website from a nondescript ranch house off Silicon Valley. Using a few hundred dollars worth of video equipment, the 33 year old Pakistani immigrant produces online lessons on maths, science and a range of other subjects which take the emphasis away from classrooms, and college campuses and are viewed by over seventy thousand students every day. In less than fifteen minutes, the Harvard educated former hedge fund manager gets to the essence of his topic: a surefire way of engaging a generation of eighteen year olds with low attention spans. There are over 1700 tutorials to choose from. Bill Gates and his 12 year old son Rory are among those who soak up the tutorials. In Facebook jargon, they're fans.

On the other side of the planet, Calvin Chin runs the peer-to-peer lending platform Qifang.com. His site caters to students, and has funded more than 3000 loans by tapping into China's cultural norms. Qifang.com asks borrowers to provide details about the family so that they feel the pressure to not let their family name down.

Up against Mary Sue Milliken of Los Angeles' Border Grill and Tracy Des Jardins of San Francisco's Jardiniere in the final of the Top Chef

Masters competition in June this year, Mumbai-born chef Floyd Cardoz dug deep into South Indian culinary traditions to whip up an unpretentious mushroom upma, a kind of semolina pudding. The top prize of USD 100,000 prize was soon his, with one of the judges, Wall Street Journal food critic Charles Passy commenting, "Cardoz won by doing exactly what he does at Tabla (his former restaurant) - by honouring his Indian gastronomic roots and finding a way to reinvent his native cuisine at the same time."

We might add: it also takes courage and pervasive creativity.

Khan, Chin and Cardoz are all brave. Even more significant is that their creativity has given them rewards. It has won them fame.

The past decade has seen an exorable shift of economic and social power eastward, towards Asia. This growth has created wealth and generated a huge mass of consumers who are rooted in tradition, yet have been subjected to social and economic upheaval and deprivation for decades.

These changes share one fundamental characteristic – more im-portant than all others – and that is the ever-growing power of ideas in Asia. We are often asked, in boardrooms, in meetings, and in interviews, "does the environment, the foundation and the ability for creativity exist in Asian societies?"

Yes. And *Raw: Pervasive Creativity in Asia* is the proof.

Raw is a rich exposition of the pervasive creativity that propels Asia. It is a celebration of native ingenuity, a compelling compilation of the evidence that Asians, rich and poor, in Communist, Islamic, democratic and ethnically diverse nations, use creativity in myriad ways. Creativity helps people solve problems. It maximises their often-limited resources. It expresses their collective identity. And, fre-quently, it generates profit.

Raw tackles head-on the idea that creativity is about genius, limited to the domain of the gifted. Instead, this book demonstrates that everybody has the capacity to be creative. Some of the best ideas are born out of collectivism rather than individualism, and this book shows that, despite accusations of being insular and self-obsessed, Asian societies have a remarkable ability to absorb new influences, mutate them and recreate them for their own benefit. It turns topsy-turvy the notion that lower order needs must be met before the human capability of higher order creativity can be unleashed. This thinking has the potential to fundamentally re-examine the need spectrum that brands are thought to satisfy.

Raw demonstrates the confidence, and sometimes the panache and swagger, of youthful Asian societies that know that their time has come. That they are no longer playing catch-up but are leading the charge. We firmly believe that it is time we gave the common, on-the-street Asian person credit for their pervasive creativity and the effect it is having on their world.

It is by paying tribute that we ourselves seek inspiration.

THE BUSINESS IMPERATIVE OF CREATIVITY

The economies of China and India continue to steam ahead with their growth levels topping 9% quarter after quarter. The economies of Indonesia, Malaysia, Pakistan and Vietnam compete to match up and sometimes exceed that growth. Thailand, South Korea and Japan strive to recover their heady domination of the 1990s. In just five years, the number of Asian brands on WPP's BrandZ top 100 most valuable brands list has risen from twelve to twenty. There can be no doubt: the 21st century will belong to Asia.

But doing business in and across Asia isn't easy, with the business environment as competitive as it is promising. The growth this time around is not illusory or a potential bubble – since the leaders in all these vibrant nations have learned, sometimes from their own mistakes, and sometimes from the experiences of others, that uni-dimensional growth, can be fraught with danger. They are now pursuing a multi-pronged approach – if India's recent successes in core manufacturing sectors and China's forays into services are any indication. It is reasonable, at this stage, to assume that this growth is sustainable and will continue to propel the economics for decades.The mass of consumers engendered by this growth has roots in tradition and experiences forged in upheaval. Many argue that this has kept them in the confines of conservatism, making them reluctant to throw open their purses in the pursuit of consumerism.

At the same time, the world has changed, as have the rules of engagement. At the turn of the century, Business Week magazine announced that the Industrial Age was over, and we had entered the Creative Age. Overlapping that transformation was what management guru Peter Drucker called The Knowledge Economy. These overlapping changes draw their force from the growing power of ideas. In an economy based on ideas rather than physical capital, the potential for the common person is far greater. Ideas, like germs, are infectious. In the Creative Age, the most important intellectual property isn't software or music or movies. It's the stuff inside employees' and consumer's heads. When assets were physical things like coal mines, shareholders truly owned them. But when the vital assets are people, there can be no true ownership. The Darwinian struggle of daily business will be won by the people - and the organisations - that adapt most successfully to this new world that is unfolding. The modern world order has been characterised by the dominance of Western innovation and creativity, while Asia, marked by the predicament of tradition, was until recently hesitant in its reaction to modern trends coming from abroad. Ten years on, the Asian century is still in the embryonic stage.

DO THE ENVIRONMENT, THE FOUNDATION AND THE ABILITY FOR CREATIVITY EXIST IN ASIAN SOCIETIES?

It seems almost absurd to even ask that question, yet there are a host of prevalent beliefs which lead many to conclude that the answer is no. India was the world's largest economy in the 16th century; China was the second largest. However, the Asian civilizations lost their primacy through colonisation, pillage, war and subsequent deprivation since the 16th century. As Europe leapt ahead, Asians lost their edge. Famine, war, religious strife and political and economic upheaval pushed entire civilisations down to the very bottom of Maslow's pyramid of needs, and they struggled to survive. Unlike the West, Asia never had an Industrial Revolution – a period that was characterised by sustained annual economic growth rates of just 0.5%, compounded year upon year. The Indians built fantastic monuments between 1500 and 1800, and the Chinese invented paper, gunpowder and circumnavigated the globe. Yet, the 20th century saw few scientific breakthroughs emerge from Asia. The essential parameters of measurement of creativity and invention – such as the Nobel Prize, the patent regime, museums and the film industry - were defined and created in the West.

By the time the Asians began to shed their colonial subjugation, they had almost lost their native capacity to create. It was more convenient to adopt Western models of development. The idea of socialism was borrowed from the Soviets, and then adapted – in India, in China, in Vietnam. The rapid changes in China are attributed to a system that has been branded 'Capitalism with Chinese Characteristics' - one where progress and growth are measured on the basis of output and consumption. Intellectual achievement continued to be defined by the number of Nobel Prizes won in the sciences, the value of art measured by prices at auctions, the box-office collections of Hollywood blockbusters and Oscar statuettes.

All of these also serve to reinforce another dimension of creativity – that it is in some way an elitist preserve, and the result of individual genius. The prevalence of the 'genius' view in contemporary western culture provides an important lens on the political economy of creativity. The genius view consists of the belief that a) creative people have unusual and phenomenal thought processes, and b) these thought processes are largely unconscious and operate through flashes of insight. Scientific studies of creative individuals, such as those done by Charles Darwin, however support just the opposite interpretation: that creative solutions are slow, incremental and involve the conscious testing and rejecting of ideas. In our experience, as we shall spell out in detail later, it is adversity and a shortage of resources that often spur creativity. Many creative solutions are not conceived in isolation but are worked out through direct or indirect contact with others. Much more than individual genius, social and cultural contexts – which are as true for Asia as for the West – serve to both nurture creativity and to evaluate and legitimate creative ideas and products.

In his book, *The Flight of the Creative Class*, Richard Florida argues that one of the greatest fallacies of modern times is that creativity is limited to a small group of people with particular talents. What is overlooked – and the most important element of his theory – is the idea that every human being is creative. By nature, we are all endowed with an incredible capacity to innovate – a result of the innate human ability to evolve and adapt. The Creative Class concept, of which Florida is the pre-eminent advocate, is a great leveler. It does not recognise the social or economic categories that we impose upon ourselves. The travesty of recent political and economic forces is that they continue to encourage the creative ability and talent of a minority and neglect the creative capacity of the masses. It is his belief that if we put three basic ideas together – that creativity is the most important source of wealth in the modern world, that every human being is creative, and that people everywhere place a high value on engaging creative work – we will witness the transformation of the world. *Raw* pursues that thesis in the Asian context.

Asians are also unfairly judged to process messages and approach problems in an overwhelmingly linear fashion, thereby further dampening creativity. Not only is this a fallacy, it is directly contrary to our natural cultural inclinations. Asia got caught up chasing the West during the tail end of the Industrial Age. Every industrial process has a beginning and an end. It follows a straight-line logic. This type of thinking is very good when you are inventing mechanical devices, because you need to think in a straight line as this is how most mathematical equations work the best. This kind of thinking also forced Asians to become task-oriented and results-driven. But Asians are not culturally disposed to think in that manner. Most Asians think in a circle. Which means, there are no lines or endings.

In a relational setting, 'circle' thinkers are much easier to get along with because of their need to be around others. Most non-linear thinking people understand they need interaction or they are missing out on their life. A life of depth and meaning comes from a multitude of intersecting circles. This is the most striking difference is between Asian and Western ways of thinking. While Western thinking strives for order, Asian thinking aspires to harmony. Rather than look for ways of reducing facts or premises into categories, eliminating what does not logically fit, it looks for ways of associating them into meaningful patterns which accommodate rather than resolve conflicting premises or facts. Associative thinking is a holistic process that looks for relationships even though no causal link is apparent. Associative thinking makes connections rather than choices. It has a greater tolerance of ambiguity and contradiction than Westerners are used to. A good example is the difference between Chinese and Ayurvedic medicine – which are holistic and symptom based, and western medicine, which is reductionist and analytic.

Asian countries are also subject to the corrosive belief that their educational systems nip the creative potential of the continent's children in the bud. Too much emphasis on rote-learning, classroom discipline, the imposition of rules, the pressures of conformity to strict norms and a measurement system entirely dependent on examinations that burden children are all cited as examples of conditions that inhibit creativity. Quite true, perhaps. But in many Asian nations, the education system was modelled after the

Western education systems of the late 19th and early 20th centuries. In societies like India, these systems replaced a far more inclusive, natural learning environment – the gurukul. In the gurukul system, students learned through their own experience as much as through the narrated experiences of their teachers. They farmed, learned the importance of piety and humility by begging for alms, and engaged with their environments on as much a spiritual as a physical level. The holistic education produced citizens who would be as proficient in warfare as in music. Even today, the *gurukul* system survives in the form of the *guru-shishya parampara* (master-student tradition) of Indian classical music. Does it stifle the sitar player's creativity? Not in the least – rather it enables a flowering of talent.

The business elite play a starring role in propagating Asian inferiority in creativity and adopting the fruits thereof. The wide gap between the US, German and Asian economies (barring Japan) in terms of earning patents is often quoted as evidence as is spending on research and development. Even in our own marketing communications industry, the number of creative awards won by agencies in the US and UK is far greater than those won by Indian, Chinese, Korean and Japanese agencies. Is this a lack of creativity at work? Certainly not. It is a failure to understand what creativity means in the Asian cultural construct.

When Western award-winning, cash-register-ringing campaigns, or their adaptations are run in Asia, they are mostly deemed to fail because 'the consumer won't get it'. The truth is, many marketing plans are based on age-old tools that fail to take into account the complexity of the Asian marketplace. Mass communications as we know it is relatively new in Asia. The commercialisation of television is only about twenty-five years old. When large populations must be reached, the mass media are assumed to be the most effective means to communicate. Customisation of messages according to cultural diversity or market need seems unnecessary looked at through this lens – if India has a billion people and China thirty percent more, that's thought to be a huge potential; as a western CEO once put it 'two and a half billion smelly armpits'.

But the Asian population has been faster to adopt technological change than many western nations. Asian consumers have turned to technology faster than their western counterparts, and in many surprising ways. Asian companies have followed suit. China has been adding a hundred million internet users every year. The number of mobile telephones in villages across Asia has outstripped fixed lines; broadband is the norm in South Korea and Japan. The new technologies make it possible to understand our consumers at a far more granular level, they have the ability to help users create and mash-up new forms of culture, and enable us to communicate with them as individuals with clear interests. Even the mass media, as the media planners would tell us, are now highly fragmented, which makes it possible to reach smaller groups with shared cultures and interests.

Senior managers who are rolled in from the west bring in cultural imperialism that inhibits the development of proper segmentation. Expat attitudes are sometimes transmitted to local managers, who argue for linear, less-adventurous communication campaigns in smaller cities: 'lower-tier China needs simple messages' a senior MNC manager recently said. The hierarchies in the corporate world coupled to a cultural deference to authority prevent junior local managers from challenging their expat superiors in many Asian markets (India is perhaps an exception). Caught up in their processes and systems – more often than not designed in and for western cultures and economies – multinational companies find it uncomfortable to keep their global learning aside and treat Asian consumers and markets as a fresh, clean slate. They get upset when a section of society refuses to fall in line with their expected beliefs, and they tend to reduce them to the lowest common denominator in terms of motivation as a result. The logic goes thus – many consumers are still struggling to meet their lower order needs of survival and safety or are caught up in their sense of belongingness. Hence they cannot move up to a higher order need for aesthetics and creativity. Marketing plans are often determined by a rigid, need-satisfaction order, according to which consumers are likely to buy those products and services that satisfy the lower order needs first. As we shall show, Maslow's hierarchy stands challenged in contemporary Asia. People are using creative strategies to meet many of their lower order needs, as much as they are willingly sacrificing their lower order needs to meet higher order ones such as self-esteem.

But there is hope. The winds of change are indeed beginning to blow. Those companies which are putting their marketing rupee, renminbi, yen or peso behind creative campaigns are finding that their bravery is fetching rewards.

You wouldn't expect State Bank of India, a large government-run financial institution to believe that financial advertising, particularly long term pension plans, could be about tapping into emotions would you? But the brave managers put their faith in a TV campaign which was based on the insight: "No matter what your age, never let money get in the way of expressing your love". The expression of this idea was a charming old man's indulgence for his wife in the form of a diamond ring as a gift on Valentine's Day. In a very touching way, it conveyed the financial empowerment one could continue to enjoy after retirement. Sales of the pension plan rose by 150%. The campaign won the Campaign of the Year award at the Advertising Club Bombay Awards (Abby's – the top creative award in India), and the Silver Effectiveness Award in 2004.

If you thought that the post office is irrelevant in today's email / text messaging / tweeting era, think again. In 2010, the chocolate brand Kit Kat created edible post cards that could be posted to children who were taking their examinations in Japan, to wish them success. They negotiated with Japan Post to offer the unique product in 22,000 post offices across Japan. The campaign was wildly successful, generating lots of free media coverage, and winning the Gold at the Asian Marketing Effectiveness Awards, and a Grand Prix at the Cannes Advertising Festival.

Raw: Pervasive Creativity in Asia is an appeal to get back to school, and get out on to the streets.

So, think of this book in terms of arguably the most famous work of structural anthropologist Claude Levi Strauss, *The Raw and the Cooked*. What we have here are the ingredients to cook up the best recipes for brands. We must pick them wisely, marinate them, mix them in the right proportions, and then light the fire of inspiration under them. Bon appétit.

Raw: Pervasive Creativity in Asia is an appeal to get back to school, and get out on to the streets.

Why do we need creativity?

Poke your head into most primary schools in India, China, Indonesia, or the Philippines and what do you hear? A soporific chant of kids repeating what the teacher has written on the blackboard. Switch on the TV set when the most popular reality show or soap opera is playing. What would you see? The same five second ad repeated ten times. Just enough to put one's nerves on edge. It starts when we're young, and it pursues us relentlessly through our entire lifetime. The same message drummed into our heads, a legacy of memorising by rote which we have not been able to shake off.

স্ট্রীট, কলিকাতা - ৭৩
DIARY DIARY
ADI
ADI
Indian Silk House
বেনারসী • সিল্ক • তাঁত
ADI
Indian Silk House
Adi
Indian
Silk
House
আদি
ইন্ডিয়ান
সিল্ক
হাউস
ADI
Indian
Silk
House
ADI
Indian
Silk
House
ADI
Indian
Silk
House

How many times does someone renting a DVD, or buying a silk saree or Lux Cozi underwear, have to be told, reminded and re-reminded that this is where you can? Apparently, plenty is not enough.

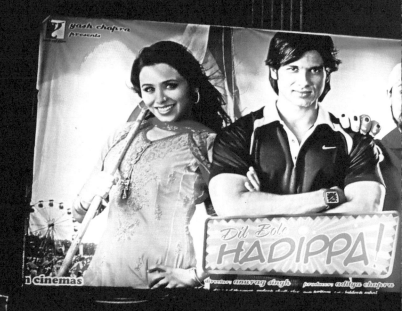

yash chopra
presents

Dil Bolo HADIPPA!

cinemas

director anurag singh   produce aditya chopra

COZI
INNERWEAR

LUX COZI
INNERWEAR

Clutter

Urban landscapes in Asia are cluttered. Businesses exist cheek by jowl, packing in all they've got within the tiniest square footage of space. Merchandise spills out of boxes on to pavements and is strung on fences and from handcarts that miraculously never topple over.

FOOD SERVICE

The GRILLE

Bakeshoppe

CENTRAL PERK

VARIEGAT

Potato Corner

TACOS Amigos

LOADING AND UNLOADING

PHILCOA
PUMILA PO LAMANG

A single lamp post hosts a myriad signs randomly pointed towards restaurants, phone booths and public toilets. The cutout of a Korean pop star rubs shoulders with a life sized model of an American Indian, wearing sunglasses.

Public space is the jostling ground for commuters and tradespeople. The rooftops of business districts are crammed with a hundred, or even more, billboards. At traffic signals, magazines, remote control covers, and key chains are thrust into car windows left ajar – all while a street kid furiously wipes the windshield with a soiled rag. This unceasing cacophony of sound and sight is the noise and fury of commerce on Asia's streets.

Competition

Creativity is a survival strategy in Asia. An average food street – Wangfujing in Beijing, Jatujak Market and Thonglor in Bangkok, or Ajmal Khan Road in New Delhi – is home to at least a hundred stalls on the pavement, which compete with local and western-style fast food restaurants. Big businesses attempt to stop customers in staid and traditional ways, like employing promoters to thrust leaflets in your hand. Small, local businesses employ more unorthodox means. The cafes of Akihabara, Tokyo dress girls up as subservient maids. Surely that is more likely to entice prospective customers!

While the shop that has the most intriguing sign or the funniest call seem to attract the attention of the passersby, those who go further and innovate with their products are able to increase their memorability. Why satisfy hunger with a regular dumpling when you can have a dozen delectable rabbits?

As competition in the job market gets fiercer by the day, youngsters across Asia are hedging their bets. When the lines outside audition centres for the Indian / Chinese / Filipino / Korean versions of 'American Idol' get as long as those outside the MBA entrance examination centre, what do some talented folks do? They set up their gig on the pavement, in city squares or in the underground, hoping that a music director or studio boss will notice them and give them a break. They don't confront their competitors; they flank them.

The manic driving that many people new to Asia rant about is a manifestation of that competition. If you don't get somewhere first, someone else will. That somewhere is often just a parking space. The business that offers its customers (sometimes misspelt as 'costumers') a few precious square-footage of asphalt is sure to earn their gratitude. Elsewhere, we find that a bank needs to secure space for the cash-delivery van, as much as it needs to secure its vaults.

44

It is such sense of competition which makes thousands of men and women risk their lives as they dart amongst the traffic trying to sell you a mobile phone charger, a duster, or the latest issue of Cosmopolitan before the light turns green. If there is someone who we should be learning from about closing a sale in 30 seconds, it is them.

Asians just have to be competitive. Thanks to the ever-burgeoning population, people seek any way they can find to differentiate themselves from the mass. Individuals and businesses must compete for attention when they are looking for work or customers, getting ahead, or even searching for partners. Small businesses thrive in these circumstances. India has spawned an entire tutoring industry because school children are compelled to excel at the university entrance exams. The coaching institutes are usually set up by graduates and PhDs from some of the same prestigious engineering and medicine schools to which the students aspire. While other engineers or those who join the academia struggle in their careers and must make do with monthly salaries, many of these coaching institute owners are millionaires. Their pedagogy is based on a deep familiarity with the pattern of questions in the entrance examinations, the influx of students fuelled by full page advertising in newspapers highlighting the stellar performance of past students.

It's the same situation in China. Schools enabling students to beat the intensely competitive gaokao system – the examination for university entrance – flourish. There's an added dimension though: parents and children like to hedge their bets. Hence, these children must learn a musical instrument, preferably the piano or the violin. As a result, the music teaching business thrives, as 30 million children tinkle the ivory and 10 million take up the bow.

Some of the best examples of creativity emerge when we examine the world of the television talent shows. As an idea itself, these shows have been imported from the west, but what makes these shows remarkable is the creative transformation of the contestants as they move up. At the risk of inviting criticism, they sometimes don personas that are essential strategies to stay ahead. Li Yuchun, the first-ever winner of China's popular Supergirl, adopted an androgynous look that instantly differentiated her from the pretty, ultra-feminine singers that Chinese viewers had hitherto encountered on CCTV.

Television channels continue to encourage contestants to dance, quiz, sing, joke, lose weight, try a hand at modelling, endure challenging conditions and cook. Thus they provide the contestants with their 15 minutes of fame and a hug from a celebrity judge. The winners get contracts, a restaurant, or an unthinkable (for the middle class anyway) sum of money.

The conditions that demand creativity in Asia

Adversity

If necessity is the mother of invention, then adversity is certainly the parent of creativity. People in Asia exhibit unparallelled ingenuity in dealing with adversity of all kinds. Frustrated by real estate hawks pestering him to sell his car repair shop – in a prime location on the streets of Manila – this shop owner added a sign making it clear he wasn't selling.

Either because they are occasional smokers, or because they don't have the money in their pocket to buy a full pack, many smokers buy their cigarettes from street-side vendors in India by the stick and light up right after buying. When the smoker walks away with a matchbox or cigarette lighter, the vendor loses more money than he makes. So what does he do? He hangs a slow-burning rope, or ties the lighter up with a wire.

A similar sense of frustration seemed to inspire the owner of a small grocery store to fashion a wooden box for his telephone, with a lock so that his employees or customers couldn't make phone calls while he was away.

On the streets of Ayutthaya, near Bangkok, this seller of fresh sweetmeats had an ingenious contraption, fashioned of old plastic bowls and bottles filled with water, to keep ants away.

In Chengdu, China, women who want to keep themselves dry when it rains and their complexion fair when the sun is out, attach umbrellas to their bicycle handlebars. Besides, their hands need to be free to maneuver through the manic traffic. If there ever was one solution to three problems, this was it.

Under obvious pressure from parents who didn't want their children to be exposed to the sun or rain, the owner ties a tarpaulin over his rickety rickshaw in Jaipur.

In India, where the harsh sun can fade the bright colours of a new car or motorcycle in weeks, their owners are quick to cover them: sometimes with a custom-made cover, sometimes with a colourful *saree* borrowed from the wife.

Dealing with the weather seems to bring out the most ingenious solutions. When it rains for weeks in Manila, local women start selling seal offerings. According to folklore, if these are offered to nuns along with a prayer, the rain will stop.

Entrepreneurs are born out of adversity.

Priyadarshini Munasinghe, or Priya, started Legacy Linen in a suburb of Colombo 15 years ago. She had performed badly at her A-levels and taken a desk job at a freight forwarding company. Intense boredom and a two-hour daily commute made her fall in love with her bed at home. It was then that she decided to start something of her own. "What?" asked her boss. "A quilt business" she replied. Her boss thought she had gone insane, but Priya had made up her mind.

Armed with her mother's old sewing machine and a few patches of fabric, she stitched her first quilt sitting in her living room. She sold it for what she believed to be the princely sum of Lankan Rupees 1,000. Using that money to borrow two more sewing machines and hiring two helping hands, she launched 'Quilter'. Her friends mockingly called her enterprise 'Quitter'. But quitting was the last thing on Priya's mind. The same friends and relatives began buying her quilts. They also brought her linen to the attention of Odel, one of the biggest department stores in Sri Lanka.

Soon a whole new world of opportunity opened up. Many of her customers - affluent Sri Lankans and expats - started demanding more than just quilts from her, and she thought that it was time to diversify her business. 'Quilter' gave way to 'Legacy Linen'.

Priya now operates from a bigger location with a team of ten. Her clientele includes the best known designer furnishing stores and boutique hotels in Sri Lanka. Wallpaper Magazine, the European style bible, rates her bed linen as one of the ten must-haves for a luxury hotel. Her work also finds mention in the Sri Lanka chapter of the Luxe City Guide. "I got to know about it from a European tourist couple who visited my workshop and showed it to me," says Priya. But she still prefers to keep a low profile and avoids the lure of mass scale production. "It'll always be quality over quantity for me," she asserts. Last year, Legacy Linen had a turnover of over Lankan Rupees 20 million. Doing badly at her examinations surely turned out to be a blessing for the company's founder.

Big business leaders face adversity, albeit of a different nature. As the example of Dr Matabee Kenji Maeda, former Chairman of Maeda Corporation in Japan shows, sheer determination and grit allowed them to seek creative solutions. Even though he headed an engineering company, Dr Maeda does not have a technical or engineering background – he is a liberal arts graduate – but he nonetheless developed a new type of concrete mixer powered by gravity. He was inspired by the method of making Japanese noodles –long his hobby. "For a long time, I had a little embarrassment about making noodles as a hobby because it gave no benefit to our business; however, for a long time I also had held this fantasy of using this noodle making skill in our real occupation, the construction business," says Dr Maeda.

One day, Dr Maeda proposed applying the theory of mixing noodle dough to mixing concrete. Unlike dough, concrete is extremely heavy and produced in large volumes – imagine the difficulty in folding and rolling out material on that scale. When he proposed this, almost all the experts in the company laughed at his idea. It seemed like too much of a leap, so naïve. The project was criticised as the 'President's Folly'. But Dr Maeda didn't give up. Five years after his original proposal, he had developed a completely new type of concrete mixer which folded the concrete in a fashion similar to how a chef uses a spatula to fold dough cooking in a wok back on itself. Through his pursuit of a disruptive technology, Dr Maeda was able to challenge convention, overcome his own adverse situation - the lack of an engineering degree - and eventually convince the sceptics.

Need for expression

As Asian societies emerge from centuries of cultural and political repression, their citizens are discovering the joy of expressing their emotions and their identity. In the process, they are carving out cultural spaces for themselves, and filling up those spaces with the new and unexpected.

In its original form, graffiti is mainly regarded as vandalism that destroys public property. It isn't surprising therefore, that in those parts of Asia obsessed with civic order, such as Singapore and China, making graffiti is illegal. Despite the law, graffiti abounds in large cities. In Chinese, graffiti is described by the colloquial word tuya which actually means 'poor handwriting, to scrawl.' This original meaning gives a degrading notion to graffiti.

In order to understand the artist's true intentions and messages, we need to place the graffiti in its context. In Beijing's 798 Art District (Dashanzi), and near Shanghai's Moganshan Road art district, graffiti is allowed to exist on the walls and in the galleries. The creators believe that they are expressing a refreshing idea in the middle of the overheated Chinese art market area - that some people were still creative without immediate financial benefits in mind.

What makes it unique is that these images are bereft of any political content, but give out social messages. The recent launch of Invasian, Asia's first magazine dedicated to graffiti, available in three languages (English, Chinese and Japanese) suggest the need to both encourage and document this form of creative expression. Bangkok even has its own dedicated graffiti website www.bkkgraff.com.

Cosplay, or 'costume play' – a kind of performance art which involves dressing up as one's favourite animation or comic-book characters – is sweeping across East Asia like wildfire. Being in a 'childlike' state is important to these individuals, because it gives them the license to be petulant, individualistic, sometimes self-centred – traits that traditional Asian societies have frowned upon and are yet deemed to be creative.

The Sword and
the Lance Subdue
the Demons II

The role models come from Japanese manga comics, Taiwanese puppet
characters and online game characters. Even as they adopt these creative,
sometimes (as the older generations describe them) bizarre persona, it is
important for their behaviour to be socially ratified. Which explains why
events such as Tokyo's Comiket, and Hangzhou's Animation Festival, originally
conceived as trade events for the promotion of the comic book and animation
industry, are such a draw with cosplayers.

There are others, like this young man riding pillion on a motorcycle in Jaipur, India, who slip on a sleeve that impersonates a tattoo.

Across cities from Chennai to Chongqing, masked parties are rising in popularity, and shops offer masks of everyone from Osama Bin Laden to Sachin Tendulkar to Angelina Jolie. The underlying impermanence of this kind of self-expression suggests that many young Asians are only experimenting with altering their identity, remaining mindful of the opinion of an older generation.

That generation is indeed the last vanguard of Asia's rich tradition. Arguably, as the proportion of seniors increases in many nations, particularly Japan and China, we have no fear of traditions being lost. Retired Chengdu and Shanghai residents don imperial costume, practice ancient traditions such as calligraphy, and play old musical instruments such as the *erhu* in public, only partly to keep themselves active. Their larger purpose is to share these arts with others and to rekindle interest.

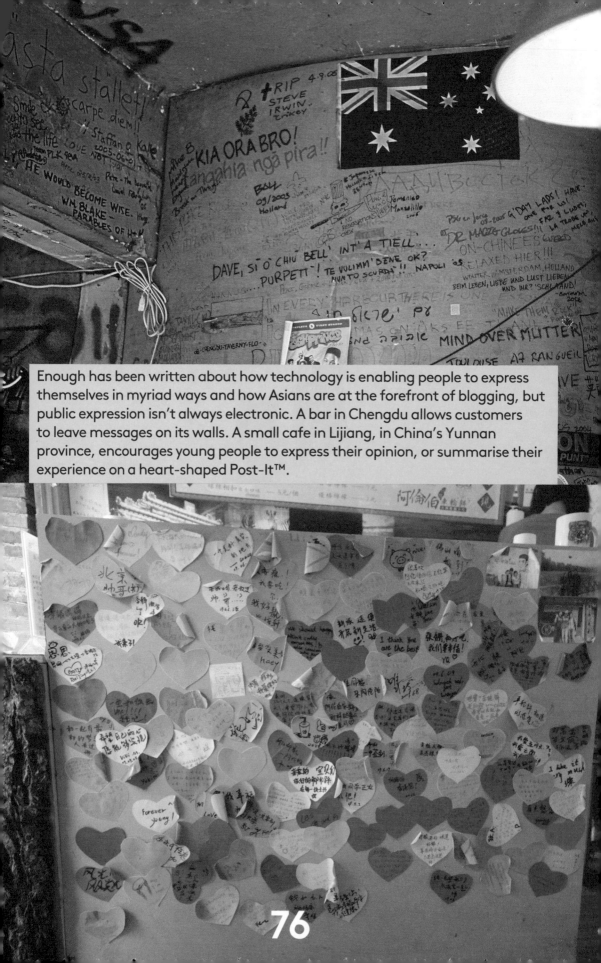

Enough has been written about how technology is enabling people to express themselves in myriad ways and how Asians are at the forefront of blogging, but public expression isn't always electronic. A bar in Chengdu allows customers to leave messages on its walls. A small cafe in Lijiang, in China's Yunnan province, encourages young people to express their opinion, or summarise their experience on a heart-shaped Post-It™.

It remains unclear, though, whether the opinion about their driving sought by taxi drivers in Manila is required by the law, or is just a smart ploy by the taxi company to suggest that they are indeed, conscious of their customer's experience. When conversations can flow both ways, creative instincts flourish.

Most religious ceremonies in Hinduism, Buddhism, Islam are not only about an individual's communion with God but also an expression of collective fervour. Religious and linguistic groups use creative expression in the form of music, art and architecture to drum up that fervour, further their appeal and inspire loyalty to a community.

Nowhere is this more evident than during the festival of Durga Puja in India's eastern metropolis, Kolkata. The festival celebrates the victory of good over evil, depicted by the slaying of the demon Mahishasura by the ten-handed Goddess Durga. For the Bengali community, this is the annual event where their neighbourhood turns into their canvas, stage and theme pavilion. In preparation for the five day festival in late autumn, traditional craftsmen in the potters' suburb of Kumartuli fashion clay idols of the Goddess, some towering ten metres high.

Each temporary temple called a *pandal* is designed by imaginative architects, usually inspired by old temples and monuments of India and sometimes by contemporary structures such as Beijing's Bird's Nest. These are then erected – usually over a bamboo structure, often using natural materials such as clay, reed, cloth and paper – only to be taken down immediately after the festival is over.

Each community competes fiercely with the rest to win the most creative *pandal* award. The awards are judged by leading figures from the creative community and sponsored by top corporations, such as Vodafone, which creates its own distinctive festival sponsorship program.

There are others who cross religious boundaries in their creative expression as they seek to establish a more secular identity. On India's Independence Day, these young Hindu girls at Varanasi's Gopi Radha Girls School sing the *qawwali*, which is a Sufi tradition.

A different kind of collective expression of creativity can be seen on Shanghai's Bund every morning. Groups of 60-year-old women tumble out of buses, change into shocking pink costumes and drum up a traditional beat whose sounds carry across the Huangpu to ultramodern Pudong. Such a marvelous spectacle!

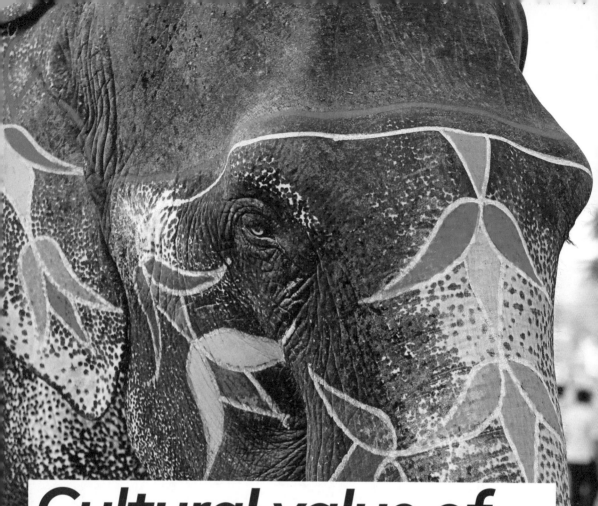

Cultural value of aesthetics

Every Asian nation, apart from Japan, is a mélange of communities and tribes. China has 55 ethnic groups, Indonesia 77, India 193, and the Philippines 180. These groups were historically differentiated by language and dialect, modes of dress and accessories. Even as many of these communities have coalesced in the modern age, they continue to adhere to significant markers of identity, mostly in the aesthetic domain.

In India and Thailand alike, elephants are adorned and worshipped, a tradition that finds its origins in the Elephant God Ganesha. The designs on an elephant can, however, change every few hundred kilometres. From a simple chalk and vermillion pattern on the streets of Jaipur to the elaborate caparisoned headgear of an elephant from the royal stables of Mysore, these designs represent the status of the owner.

Over the centuries, common folks adapted the grandiose cultural celebrations of their rulers in their personal way. During the Dussehra festival, when colourful, giant effigies of the demon God Ravana are burnt in public grounds (erstwhile palace grounds), those who can't be part of the spectacle celebrate in a modest way by burning their own effigies. Small effigy makers, like this one in Jaipur's Chawri Bazar, have thrived as a business for hundreds of years.

On these same streets, craftspeople have woven umbrellas for just as long. Except that these intricately embroidered masterpieces are no longer bought for daily use. Instead, they adorn the living rooms of India's growing middle class. Elsewhere, as in Thailand, umbrellas take on a ceremonial meaning. They are brought out during processions and funerals, and these seven, five and three tiered royal umbrellas are collectively known as *Apiroom Chum Sai*.

This aesthetic culture imbues objects of everyday use with colour and beauty. In the ancient town of Kashgar, on China's border with Kyrgyzstan, markets are piled high with everything from chests for carrying back and storing one's wedding dowry, to flower vases, snuff boxes and containers for dry fruit.

Everything, it seems, can be turned into an object of beauty. In Qibao, a small watertown in suburban Shanghai, a sweetmeat seller warms up sugar candy and shapes it into animals and dragons before it solidifies. Two shops away a young woman paints *Kunqu* opera faces and watertown scenes on eggshells, and then frames them up for sale as souvenirs.

On the streets of Seoul, a seemingly mundane wooden top is infused with colour.

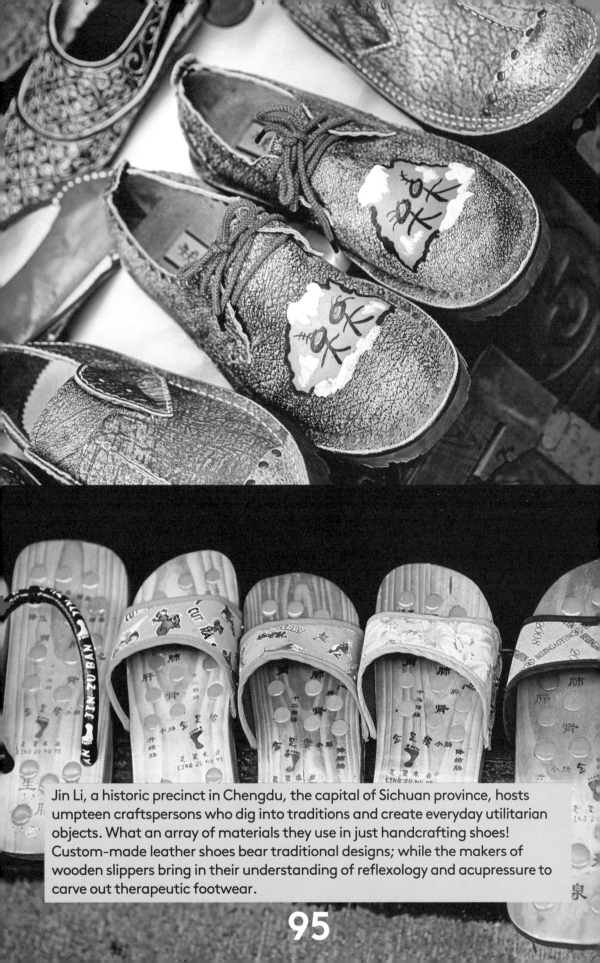

Jin Li, a historic precinct in Chengdu, the capital of Sichuan province, hosts umpteen craftspersons who dig into traditions and create everyday utilitarian objects. What an array of materials they use in just handcrafting shoes! Custom-made leather shoes bear traditional designs; while the makers of wooden slippers bring in their understanding of reflexology and acupressure to carve out therapeutic footwear.

The ballet-like silk slippers worn by a middle-aged lady are rich with the designs of Chinese tapestry. The same lady is quite likely to carry her loose change in a coin purse made of reed or grass, embellished with flowers, and hang a mask accessory from her mobile phone.

98

男きもの
ちどり屋

鷺
娘

In Japan, aesthetics often take three different forms: *Yûgen*, which draws from nature and emphasises profound grace and subtlety, *geido*, which echos back to the traditional Japanese arts of calligraphy, floral arrangement and theatre, and *iki*, which describes the aesthetically appealing qualities that, when applied to a person, constitute a high compliment. Paintings on these doors draw liberally from these traditions.

Hinduism, with its myriad ceremonies and 330 million Gods and Goddesses, is a particularly expressive religion. Since many worshippers find it difficult to visit the temple regularly, they surround themselves with images of some of these deities – such as around the entrance door of a home in Kolkata. They place miniature brass images of Gods (like the Cowherd God Krishna) decorated with silk and tinsel, in their shops, on the bedroom mantelpiece, in the kitchen, and always in sight.

In countries with a dominant Christian population, such as in the Philippines, Jesus appears emblazoned on buses and jeepneys. Riding them can always bring out a prayer.

If the popularity of good luck charms on the streets of Asia are any indication, the 'higher powers' only give you a hearing when you use some creative ways to communicate. Talk about using creativity to break through the clutter! Necklaces, amulets, fiery dragons are all guaranteed to drive one's worries away, especially if the charms are made by a monk.

The ancestors of Jaipur's blue pottery artisans learned their craft from Mongol masters in the 14th century. An art that began as a way of decorating tombs, mosques and palaces was adapted 500 years later by the once-conquered population of Hindus to produce decorative household goods such as urns, vases, tea sets, jugs and napkin rings. Today, wealthy businessmen use the same blue glazed floral motifs throughout their homes from the grand entrances to their bathrooms.

Such patronage of creativity, which also takes the form of traditional paintings such as that of several women coalescing to form the image of an elephant drawn directly on the wall, keeps the kilns burning and the artists looking for braver ways of expressing their creativity.

Every now and then, the melody of street music drowns the noise and bustle of Asian streets. In Chengdu, a *qipao* clad girl plucks away a folk song on a *guqin*, hoping to lure passersby into the restaurant that values (and profits from) her talent.

In Delhi's old city, the one-string *ektara*, musical instrument of the wandering minstrel, is sold by a street salesman who can perhaps play only a tune or two but hopes to kindle the talent of many starry-eyed youngsters, for only ten rupees.

The National Folk Museum
of Korea
國立民俗博物館

Since 1945

국립민속박물관

Eager to preserve and promote the value of this aesthetic culture, city authorities are demarcating historic precincts and encouraging their preservation. Here, old buildings are refurbished as modern cafes, boutiques, music stores and as museums.

In and around Chengdu's Jinli Street, we find building exteriors embellished with golden blooms and mundane door handles have no place amidst the exquisite patterns in carved redwood and crystal.

Shanghai's leafy French Concession and the historic Bund are filled chock-a-block with Art Deco buildings that bear the city government's stone plaque certifying their authenticity and heritage.

优 秀 历 史 建 筑
HERITAGE ARCHITECTURE

高安路14号

原为阿麦仑公寓。砖混结构，1941年竣工。现代派风格。平面依道路转角呈弧形。立面两端设大阳台，顶部设遮阳薄板。室内装饰简洁精致，5、6层为跃层布置。

Amyron Apartments. Completed in 1941. Brick-and-concrete composite structure. Modern style.

上海市人民政府 1994年2月15日公布
Shanghai Municipal Government Issued on 15th Feb. 1994

111

11

In their urge to differentiate themselves, some youngsters hark back to the past and choose to don fashions of the yesteryears when they get their portfolios shot. There's evidently greater charm for them in royal and court regalia, as they forsake the so-called simplicity of modern style for the elaborate, colourful costumes of a bygone era. These examples show that the very population that is frequently labelled as uncreative and unimaginative actually belongs to an extraordinarily rich culture, one that refuses to fade despite the onslaught of modernity.

Tourist destinations are some of the best showcases for local talent. Many Chengdu teahouses such as Shunxing Old Teahouse stage nightly Sichuan opera and musical performances. For 90 minutes, viewers are immersed in a fluid choreography, an art that is learned and refined over generations.

Every evening, on board the Victoria Empress, cruising the mighty Yangtze upstream from Yichang to Chongqing, the front desk and waitstaff exchange their uniform for opera costumes. One accomplished star from amongst them engages holidaymakers with her face-changing stunt. In the time it takes to flip a fan across her face, she changes her masks from angry to sad, from delight to desperation.

The National Museum in Seoul houses the Korean equivalent of the Mona Lisa — a bronze figure called 'The Pensive Bodhisattva' which is both beautiful and moving. That it is not as well known as Leonardo's painting is a reminder of the lesser importance given to Asian art in the world and emblematic of a continuing dominance of Western art movements in Asia. This is evident in the outpouring of new public sculptures in Seoul, which comes as a result of a Korean law requiring commercial buildings to spend a percentage of their construction budget on the arts. Most of it is in the 'international modern' sculpture style that is increasingly seen in most Asian countries. Having achieved considerable economic and industrial development, they now seek to become an international centre for the arts. A country that is the best in the world in terms of the value and place of arts and culture in their society is just as worthy an aim as economic dominance.

Says Dong-chea Chung, former Minister of Culture and Tourism for South Korea, "I believe that art is closely linked to our everyday lives, and I believe in the positive value which art brings to all aspects of our lives. In this respect, I think 'arts education' plays a role in helping a process that people experience, put together and reorganise various factors of their lives."

Two other arts infrastructure initiatives stand out in South Korea. One, the state-initiated Gwangju project where USD 1.8 billion are being invested in developing 'A Culture Hub City of Asia', which will become the 'ground of exchanges, culture creation, studies and education for a peaceful Asia in the future, where culture becomes the engine for economic development'. Two, the Korean Business Council for the Arts (KOBCA) that fosters co-operation between businesses and arts communities with the aim "to enhance the interest and the understanding of the Korean people in culture and the arts, as well as contribute to the balanced development of business and the arts".

Kim Koo, one of the founding fathers of modern Korea, wrote in his essay 'My Desire' in 1947: "I want our nation to become the most beautiful nation in the world. I do not want our nation to become the richest and most powerful nation in the world. Because I have felt the pain of being invaded by another nation. I do not want my nation to invade others. It is sufficient that our wealth is such that it makes our lives abundant and our military strength such that it is able to repel others' invasion. The only thing that I desire in infinite quantity is the power of a highly-developed culture. This is because the arts both makes us happy and gives happiness to others. I am convinced that this will be accomplished by our strength and, particularly, by the power of education."

In contemporary Asia, a combination of government and business is finding ways of taking creativity to the public – a throwback to the era when Asian societies were ruled by monarchs whose mission was to create monuments, works of art and music, even cities. Under their patronage, creative people found fame and fortune (if you discount what Emperor Shah Jehan ordered for the craftsmen who built the Taj Mahal. He had their hands cut off, so that no one could create a similar monument ever after. It was a form of protecting intellectual property, albeit cruel.)

The authenticity of tribal artists has immense value. Bhajju Shyam is one such artist. He grew up watching his mother paint the walls of their home but displayed no inclination to paint himself. At 16, he left his village for Bhopal, the capital of the Indian state of Madhya Pradesh, where he began working as a night-watchman until his uncle, a well-known Gond artist, took him under his wing. Bhajju's natural talent, nurtured by his environment, took flight and his works began to be noticed. When a restaurateur in London invited Bhajju to paint the interiors of his restaurant, Bhajju used his free time to paint London's landmarks in his inimitable Gond style. The London Jungle Book, based on his paintings became a hit in the art circles. WPP noticed his work, and commissioned him to design the 2005 Annual Report – which in turn picked up several major design awards.

In Mumbai, the Kala Ghoda Arts Festival is organised by the city authorities around the Jehangir Art Gallery every year. This vibrant smorgasbord of street art, performances and installations is a celebration of expression. The area itself – named after the statue of a horse on which King Edward VIII mounted - has a distinct visual identity. Over 100,000 square feet of existing indoor gallery space, mass outdoor pavement galleries, and exhibition space within the covered arcades, make the area a living, breathing urban museum.

As a legacy of centuries of invasion and foreign rule in many parts, Asians have learned to absorb new ideas and influences, combining them with their own sensibility. The current invasion is mostly cultural, and it is omnipresent – from supremely popular adaptations of talent shows like 'American Idol', to cuisine, to the ubiquity of schoolbags emblazoned with Disney characters (and now Hello Kitty and Pleasant Sheep).

Even as Disneyland draws in the crowds in Tokyo and Hong Kong, Disney-style amusement parks are sprouting up in the outskirts of most cities. Two hours from Manila sprawls Fantasy World, a part Jurassic Park, part Animal Kingdom wonderland, where families who can't afford the short overseas flight troop in on weekends.

Indeed, Mickey Mouse reigns as America's most valuable export. From being painted on the steps leading up to a kindergarten in old Jaipur, to intercity buses in Thailand, he makes his influence well known. But when he makes an attempt to enter the bathrooms printed on a towel, Mickey faces some stiff competition from that other mouse – Jerry. Spiderman is muscling in too.

Spiderman also spins his web above a shopping mall in Bandung, Indonesia, where he is joined in his quest to protect humanity by Superman.

Rambo lends his name to a jeans shop, as he straddles above the entrance ready with his rocket launcher. Rambo also visited the Manila Zoo, with a stag draped over his muscular shoulders (what a switch from a rocket launcher!)

Superman, muscles rippling, is enjoying the ambiance in a bar called 'The Filling Station' in Manila. Even he needs a refill, sometimes. Across the floor, Elvis croons.

The fascination for the foreign doesn't stop at contemporary icons or cultural symbols. While nations like India and China have no dearth of fortresses and castles – fantastic creations in their own right – what seems to catch the fancy of the young are European-style, turreted castles, fortresses with moats, and windmills. DIY kits flood the marketplace, and the finished pop-up models occupy pride of place in the living rooms of the middle class.

PINK

3D PU

WINDMILL FARM

3Druze Mushroom Fairyland

FUNNY

3Druze WINDMILL FARM

uild your own Opera House

PUZZLE

133

映画史上不朽의 大浪漫篇! 完璧의配役에 豪華絢爛의 大画幅을展開!
總天然色
CINEMASCOPE
지나·로로부리지다 主演
안소니 · 퀸
文豪빅토르·유-고原作 巨匠장·드라노와監督
노틀담의 꼽추

The notion of romance is timeless and, dubbed or subtitled into Korean, may just as easily be inspired by Gone With the Wind, La Dolce Vita and Roman Holiday, as Pretty Woman or When Harry Met Sally.

The notion of the open society came originally from philosopher Karl Popper in a book written during the Second World War, The Open Society and Its Enemies. In that time of global distrust, politicians and generals found it convenient to build the Berlin Wall, put up the Iron and the Bamboo Curtain, and then found it necessary to send in unmanned spy planes to find out what was going on behind the wall. Throughout history, closed societies often scored early victories, but they tend to lack staying power. Their people are stirred to great efforts only by compulsion and propaganda. They have no creative incentive - only the negative ones of escaping punishment or harassment. As the totalitarian regimes collapsed, as communications and trade linked faraway societies, the incentive for the people to connect and create has returned. In many ways, Asia is at the forefront of that change and one of its prime beneficiaries. Asian nations and their leaders have chosen their paths to the future in ways that are remarkably different from western models of progress and governance.

There is, moreover, diversity within Asia itself. The political systems in China and India are polar opposites, and Taiwan, South Korea, Singapore and Malaysia make remarkable economic progress under authoritarian regimes. While in Thailand and Pakistan, the military plays an important role, Vietnam continues to be a communist nation. But all of them are remarkable growth stories – which may be attributed in good measure to the economic and cultural openness of the people, be it leaders in the government, business or the general public. In the 21st century, governments have realised that they can do little to contain the ambitions of the people.

Having suffered poverty and deprivation for generations, the people in Asia want to get rich. They will go anywhere where opportunity and fortune awaits them – be it Chinese restaurateurs in Venice, Indian software programmers in Silicon Valley, Bangladeshi food merchants in London, Filipino maids in the Middle East, or Japanese politicians in Peru.

By their very nature, Asians are opportunists, and in the open society, talent will go wherever there is opportunity. They can adapt to any environment, even as they retain their cultural moorings. It is this trait that makes them remarkably creative. Asian writers do well at the Man Booker prizes because they write about their native cultures, giving the English language a flavour that is unique. Some are calling this phenomenon 'The Empire Strikes Back'. Asian music – from Korean and Japanese pop, to Bhangra and Qawwali - is sweeping the world because of its distinctive sound. The designs of Vivienne Tam and Issey Miyake stand out on the catwalks because of their Asian sensibilities, and in turn inspire a million others to follow the path.

A team of architects - Ma Yansong, Yosuke Hayano, Dang Qun – better known as MAD Architects, from Beijing won a prestigious competition to build the Absolute Towers in Mississauga, Canada. The building's striking curvaceous form prompted locals to dub it as the Marilyn Monroe Tower. When Louis Vuitton emblazoned its handbags with Takeshi Murakami's manga designs, there were long queues outside its flagship store in Paris. Hewlett Packard collaborated with Vivienne Tam to design its notebooks, and she drew inspiration from the classic Chinese story 'Butterfly Lovers'. The 1980s and 1990s provided the turning point for many Asians to unleash their creative potential and turn it into business advantage.

An accountant at a food company pushed a snack cart to the front gate of Window to the World, a theme park in Shenzhen, Guangdong Province, to sell Japanese-style noodles. In eight days, she had racked up more than USD 20,000 in sales, and went on to win the franchise for Japan's Ajisen Ramen's restaurants. Ten years later, when Ajisen China went public with an IPO, the issue was oversubscribed by 192 times. Poon Wai, the handcart pusher, owns 51% of the company. During the Cultural Revolution in China, Tong Zhi Cheng worked at a state-owned piano factory that had dirt floors. He had to load pianos on a handcart and push them to the dockyards of Shenzhen.

He is now the Chairman of Pearl River Piano, the same company, which is the largest piano manufacturer in the world making 100,000 pianos a year, exporting worldwide and encouraging 30 million students in China to learn the instrument. Had there been no free trade, as mandated by the WTO and stimulated by the open society, Cheng's factory would still be making a hundred pianos a year. Filmmaker Ning Hao, whose film Crazy Stone was a runaway success at the box office in 2006, admits that Guy Ritchie and Quentin Tarantino are his 'teachers'. His first film was inspired by Philip Kaufman's 'The Unbearable Lightness of Being'. When you watch Ning Hao's films, you do realise that he is indeed seeking inspiration, but certainly not copying them. Inspiration and opportunity are the hallmarks of the open society.

In the book, Very Thai, Siamologist Niels Mulder is quoted saying, "Eclectic borrowing, temporisation, adaptive skill and pragmatism are the very flavour of the Thai cultural genius. They trust their own ways; meanwhile they are not shy to incorporate whatever is perceived as useful or attractive." Ronald McDonald with folded hands is a wonderful example of the pragmatism that local management of the fast-food chain exhibits when it operates in Thailand, as indeed, in the rest of Asia. This is the biggest legacy of the open society. As organisations are discovering, multi-cultural teams are best at the cross-fertilisation of ideas. Combined with the resurgence of cultural pride, Asians across the socio-economic spectrum are allowing their creativity to flower, and the world is beginning to notice.

Creative strategies

How do common people come up with such uncommon, unique ideas? By looking into their immediate surroundings, by adopting un-expected pathways, and by combining wit, wisdom and willpower into an irresistible whole. It is well docu-mented that Westerners are more likely to insist on using formal logic, while Asians are willing to live with more contradiction. The Western style is to state things clearly and directly so that no misunderstanding is possible, while the Asian communication style is less direct and less clear, to Westerners at least.

This idea is at the heart of the preeminent strategy Asians adopt when they need things done – obliquity. Strange as it may seem, overcoming geographic obstacles, winning decisive battles or meeting global business targets are the type of goals often best achieved when pursued indirectly. Oblique approaches are most effective in difficult terrain, or where outcomes depend on interactions with other people. If you want to go in one direction, the best route may involve going in the other. Paradoxical as it sounds, goals are more likely to be achieved and achieved faster when pursued the long way around.

Guanxi is an indigenous Chinese construct and is defined as an informal, personal connection between two individuals who are bound by an implicit psychological contract to follow a series of social norms including maintaining a long-term relationship, mutual commitment, loyalty and obligation. A quality guanxi is also characterised by the mutual trust and feeling developed between the two parties through numerous interactions following the principles of self-disclosure and dynamic reciprocity. In China, most difficult problems can be resolved through guanxi. It is an indirect creative strategy that relies on human relationships, not business ethics. It has been cultivated over centuries, because what the civilisation had in abundance was social, not economic, capital. In contemporary China, ironically, it is now used to build economic capital.

Obliquity reigns in India as well. Despite the meritocracy that the nation aspires to, most things work because of the strong ties in existing relationships. When a father has to convey his disapproval to his son or daughter, he often chooses to do it through the mother to soften the blow. In many traditional families, women never address their husbands directly by their name, referring to them as their son or daughter's father Gudiya ke Papa. In the highly competitive workplace, all things being equal, the job goes to the applicant who is more likely to have some social or family connections with the boss. Arranged marriages are still the norm, and the credibility of the prospective bride or groom must be established through the opinions of neighbours or colleagues, and never through direct questioning of the prospect. Even when romantically inclined, few Indian youths can muster up the courage to ask a girl or boy out – they first go through an elaborate ritual of finding out, through the social network, if the object of their affection is interested.

Obliquity finds further purchase in the very language that Asians speak. The rich metaphors that pepper the languages of Asia are not confined to classical texts. Rather, they are used in everyday conversation and often drawn from nature. Metaphors serve to avoid stating something directly or to make a suggestion.

For example, in China, if an older, more experienced person has to make a younger person pay heed to his or her advice, s/he would say "Wo chi guo de yan bi ni chi guo de fan hai duo." ("I have eaten more salt than you have eaten rice."). It's like saying, 'I am old enough to have more knowledge and experience than you.' Or, in Indonesia, when they refer to the generation gap, they say: "Bagai pinang dibelah dua." ("Intergenerational communication is like an areca nut divided into two.") Implying that though two may be from the same family, they are now too far apart. Koreans emphasize family values by saying: "Namuae Gajiga Maneulsuruk, Duh Maneun Baramyi Bubnida." ("The more branches a tree has, the more wind it attracts.")

When former President of China Jiang Zemin was asked about US-China relations, he said: "Gu zhang nan ming" ("Clapping with one hand produces no sound") implying that the US had to take steps to improve relations. Indians use the same proverb, saying "Ek haath se taali nahi bajti."

To all those who insist on direct, linear com-munications for their brands in Asia we posit: if in their everyday lives, people are used to indirect, often metaphorical communications, why does brand communications have to be any different? After all, people use creative strategies everyday to better their lives and further their businesses.

Resourcefulness

This is the spirit of *jugaad*, or making do. Across north India, villagers bolt a diesel generator to a chassis, latch on a discarded truck or tractor transmission, and lo and behold, you have public transport! This vehicle is called just that – a *Jugaad*.

Next to a waterfall in Sulawesi, Indonesia, an entrepreneur rents out old, inflatable tyre innertubes to teenagers eager for a ride. Children in the backstreets of Manila cobble together a basketball hoop for a game.

In Delhi, a mom and pop store owner bolts a discarded part of a photocopy machine to a plastic stool, to serve as a base for a pay phone.

In Tokyo, where money is not usually a constraint, old water bottles are cut away and fashioned into cats by a boutique owner. A retailer of surfer chic brand Quiksilver creates his own mobile promo vehicle by attaching a pair of surfboards to a *tuktuk*.

The same kind of mobility is exhibited by two fortune tellers on a Seoul sidewalk, as they set up a rain-sheltered booth wherever they think their customers are likely to be. Rattan screens provide a semblance of privacy to their clients in what is a very public space.

A similar concern for his passengers motivates the *tuktuk* driver in Jaipur to stitch together four sheets of jute cloth to protect them from rain. The cloth, naturally, comes from potato sacks. But the security guard in Manila is only concerned about not getting himself wet when he straps on a small umbrella to his head. At least his hands are free to direct traffic into the office compound whose gate he minds!

To suggest how fresh his stock of fruit was, a vendor in one of Manila's wet markets hung his stock of bananas from a faux banana tree.

There are yet others whose ideas are more to do with embellishment of the ordinary than to find solutions to problems. On the streets of Ayutthaya, near Bangkok, a bicycle owner had customised his vehicle using flattened beer cans, which was such a wonderful reminder of the Temple of a Million Beer Bottles – *Wat Pa Maha Chedi Kaew*, built by monks in northeast Thailand.

Asian communities share strong relationships with their physical and social environments. Having lived in poverty for much of their recent history, they are perhaps more acutely aware of the need to maximise their available resources than are those who live in the developed world.

They are, for example, remarkably adept at drawing more than the expected value out of natural resources. In Malaysia, taxi drivers use fragrant pandan leaves to keep their vehicles smelling fresh all day. No artificial, canned air fresheners for them. Long before 'environmental sustainability' was such a buzz phrase, Asians were cooling their drinks in mountain streams and using the bubbling hot springs to cook rice.

Where most work still gets done by raw physical power, they are constantly looking for and inventing ways of minimising that effort. If you logged on to YouTube and keyed in 'Mr Wu Robots', you will find the fascinating account of a certain Mr Wu who lives in a village in China, but designs robots out of scrap. While some of them do more entertaining things like dance, one ponderously pulls a rickshaw and takes Mr and Mrs Wu shopping. During winter, many Chinese motorcyclists fix leather or rubber tubes to their bike handlebars. It saves them money required to buy gloves, and the bother of remembering to pick them up wherever they go.

In the north Indian state of Punjab, ingenious road-side restaurant 'dhaba' owners use top-loading washing machines to churn milk to make buttermilk. Mohammad Saidullah, a villager, has developed an amphibious bicycle. This contraption mates a conventional bicycle with four rectangular air floats to support the bicycle when moving in water. Fan blades are attached radially to the spokes of the rear wheel, enabling it to run on both water and land.

Opportunism

Nothing exemplifies the spirit of opportunism more than the firm conviction that the pavement is the marketplace. Accosting passersby, shifting their business according to their prospects' moves, the pavement is the production line, demonstration booth and sales counter all rolled into one. Every afternoon, just before the closing bell rings at the Town4Kids kindergarten in Jakarta, the bubble-blower appears and starts peddling his wares.

The *golgappa wallah* is an itinerant snack seller who roams residential neighbourhoods of every town in north India in the early evening with his vessels filled with spicy treats, eager to satisfy the cravings of hungry families. The kids have perhaps just returned from their playtime, the man of the house may have just returned from work but the lady is too tired to rustle up a snack. So this is his moment, entirely.

Just before the border crossing between Gurgaon and Delhi (where, unlike Gurgaon, it is compulsory to wear a helmet), helmet sellers wheel in their trolley and set up shop along the highway. Sometimes business is good, and sometimes not. That's when the shop owner takes a nap in the shade of his wares.

For many of these pavement entrepreneurs, regardless of what they might be selling, having a set of wheels under their carts is an absolute necessity.

The size of those wheels may be different, as the banana seller in Manila, the souvenir seller in Ayutthaya, the cacti seller and snack vendor in Chengdu illustrate, but they serve the common purpose of enabling a fast getaway when the authorities come-a-calling.

The craftswomen in Jaipur's old city have no such concerns, especially before Diwali, the festival of lights. The city values their native pottery so they occupy the entire pavement, which now serves as their workshop and studio. The hot sun bakes the clay, whereupon they paint the festive lamps and piggy banks in the traditional colours of red and gold.

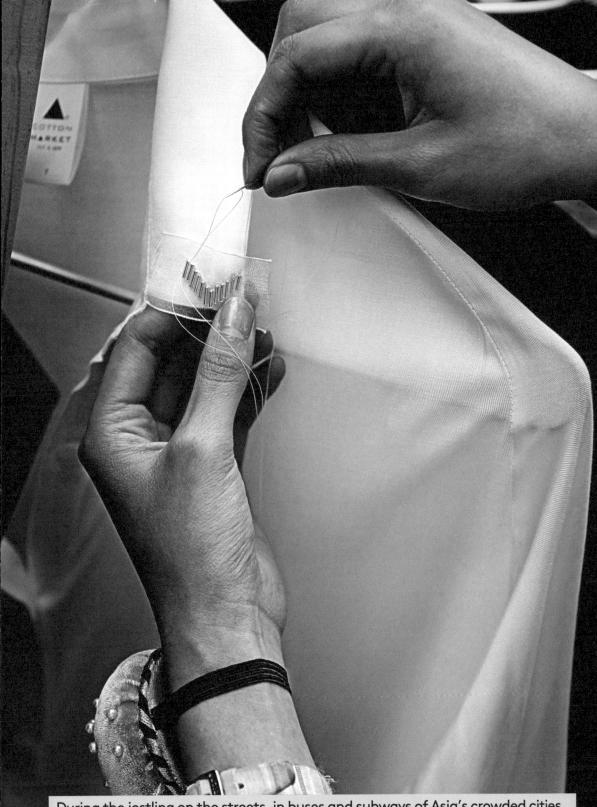

During the jostling on the streets, in buses and subways of Asia's crowded cities, it is perhaps quite natural for a zipper on one's bags to come unstuck, or to lose a button on a shirt. That's where the fixers step up, repairing everything on the spot. Whether it is in Jaipur or in Seoul, they provide a service that is as invaluable as it is opportunistic.

Physical mobility is a key characteristic of small entrepreneurs across Asia. Consider the dabbawallas of Mumbai. Now recognised as a classic business case study of just-in-time management, they invented it much before the Japanese thought of it. For a fee of about 300 rupees a month (USD 6), these men pick up lunchboxes from the homes of office-goers at about 10 am in the morning (on an average, two hours after he leaves home – giving the missus more time to cook) and deliver them exactly in time for lunch break. Not one dabba (tiffin-box) is ever misplaced – thanks to a system of codes that only they fathom, and the whole system works like a well-oiled machine. At the end of lunch hour, the dabbas are dutifully collected and delivered back home late by the afternoon. The entire system rakes in a few million dollars annually, and keeps thousands employed.

Of late, the *dabbawallas* are being used by smart direct marketing companies to deliver targeted promotional materials. Want to reach only the financial district? They will deliver to Dalal Street's army of sharebrokers. On a much larger scale, the stall owners at the village markets (*haats* as they're called in India and Bangladesh) all over rural Asia move from one village to another selling their goods. They go where opportunity beckons, piling their merchandise onto handcarts. Sometimes four or five traders share a tractor trolley.

Entrepreneurship

Harvard Business School professor Tarun Khanna writes in his book, *Billions of Entrepreneurs*, that the Indians and the Chinese have business opportunism almost hardwired into their genes and culture. According to the Organisation of Economic Cooperation and Development (OECD), small and medium-sized enterprises account for more than 90% of all firms outside the agricultural sector and constitute a major source of employment in Asia. Our journey through the streets of Asia provides ample proof of that spirit.

The streetside craftsperson is a creative soul and businessperson rolled into one, quick to spot emerging market needs. The popularity of Ninja characters on the screen and in comic books prompted one such entrepreneur in Bangkok to create an array of his own.

Age does not dim their ability. Paper wheels that delight children, animal figures fashioned out of dry grass, colourful pouches made out of silk and velvet that young fashionistas might carry to a party – all in a day's work as these 70-year-olds wield their needle, pliers and brush with aplomb in Ayutthaya and Jakarta.

A young man gives them competition when he designs swinging monkeys that would perhaps rest on the window of a 10-year-old's room. They are all tapping into the desire of a fast-growing middle class eager to do up their home, perhaps only recently bought.

The homeless man in Jaipur, who creates decorative horses, is serving the same need. He crafts these fanciful animals out of leftover fabric pieces donated by a local factory. One large sheet of cloth serves as his makeshift roof, right next to the road that is his 'showroom'.

Further down the same road, a potter takes up a good part of the streetside to set up his own shop, selling planters, flower vases, mugs and bathroom accessories. Right next to him, there's another man selling seats made out of tightly bound reed. No wonder, many Indians joke that you can buy anything on a city's pavement, but you can't walk.

On Khao San Road, Bangkok's famed backpacker precinct, a street vendor hangs windchimes and trinkets made from dried bottle gourd. Another sells colourful fish ornaments, and yet another man creates dreadlocks for wannabe hippies while wearing one of his own creations.

สมศักดิ์ทำฟัน

(เจ้าเก่า)

รับทำฟันปลอม
และรับซ่อม
ฟันคลอม ฟันเห่าง

With a history going back at least 100 years, the artisan of dentures and false teeth fills a useful niche, albeit technically illegal, in the world of Bangkok teeth. On Maharat Road, these false teeth makers even offer dentures for pet canines. When the waiting list at a dentist is too long – sometimes two years for dental crowns – the customer comes here. They charge 200 baht for a single false tooth, 800 baht for a false canine tooth, 2,000 baht for a fashionable dental crown and 2,500 to 7,500 baht for a full set of dentures.

ประธานทำฟั...

ในซอยร้านขายหนังดอกหญ้า ท่าพระจัน...

ซ่อม ฟันปลอม ทำฟันปลอมทุกช...

โครงโลหะ พลาสติกตกไม่แ...

(ประสบการณ์มากกว่า 20 ปี)

Tel : 081-832-603...

การฝากไม้มงคล 9 อย่าง
รักซ้อน มะรุม มะยม ขนุน
กาหลง พยูง ยอ มะขาม คูณ
พ่อท่านเขียน วัดกระทิง

...ฝากก ลิ้นฟ้า ยอ มะรุม

The Bangkok entrepreneur doesn't stop at dentures. At Wat Mahathat, the city's biggest amulet market, vendors thrive on people's insecurities. Amongst their most popular wares is the *palad khik*, or the penis amulet worn by men in their underclothes to ensure potency. The charm's powers evidently transcend gender, because it was reported that Papasara Techapaiboon, wife of former cabinet minister Pornthep Techapaiboon, is reputed to have hidden a small one in her hair when she was crowned Miss Thailand World in 1998. The Bangkok Post says that the production of these amulets is a multi-million baht business.

In Chengdu, one street vendor takes her local popcorn to her customers when she braves the traffic on her hand-drawn cart. The giant plastic bags keep her wares fresh and dry, even as they allow her prospective customers to see what she's selling.

185

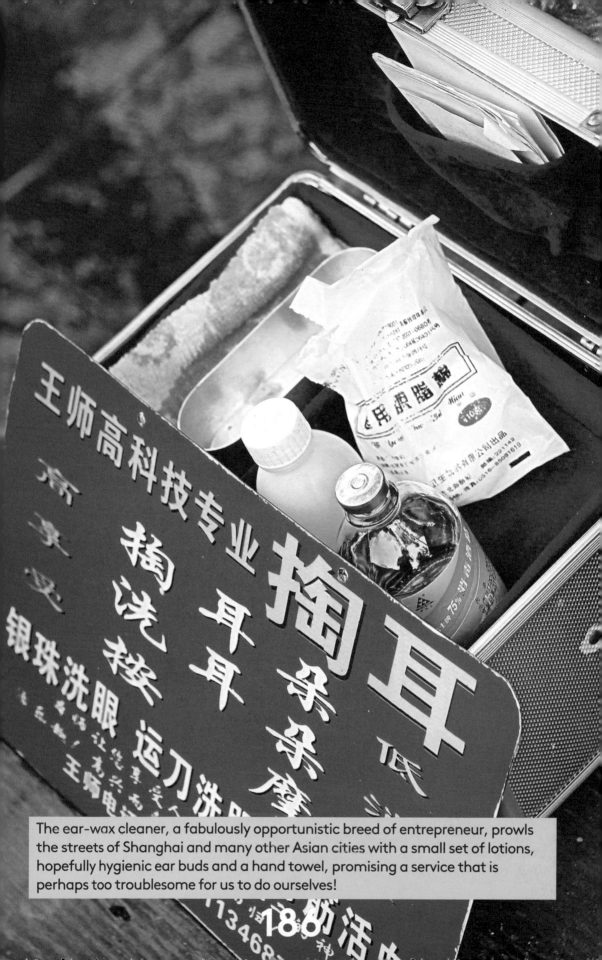

王师高科技专业掏耳

高享受

挖洗耳朵

银珠洗眼 运刀洗眼

王师电

The ear-wax cleaner, a fabulously opportunistic breed of entrepreneur, prowls the streets of Shanghai and many other Asian cities with a small set of lotions, hopefully hygienic ear buds and a hand towel, promising a service that is perhaps too troublesome for us to do ourselves!

On the streets of Delhi, the seller of liquid sustenance mixes it up quite well by placing bottled soft drinks and water on his cart, but his signage proclaims he's selling fresh fruit juice. Depending on what his clients need, he either wields a bottle-opener or presses the buttons on his blender-juicer.

Natsuki Matsuda is a Japanese entrepreneur in Shanghai's French Concession who runs a rather unique store called Ushigokoro, meaning 'cow's heart'. The 25 square metre shop is crammed with 170 small wooden boxes. She rents these wooden boxes out to local artists and designers for a small fee allowing them to display and sell their work. Small boxes means small products, and as a result, there's a cheap and cheerful jumble of jewelry, art work and other hand-crafted knick-knacks for sale. The only condition she has is that whatever's on sale here should not be available anywhere else, and must be self-produced.

And in Tokyo, Yoshitake Tanaka is a celebrity ice cream seller who designed the façade of his store as an ice cream truck. His Hanabatake Bokujo (Flower Garden Ranch) Cafe offers raw caramel candy, ice cream, cheese, and pudding out of a faux bright pink ice cream truck, with flowers on the windshield, which certainly stands out in Tokyo's commercial jungle.

It is this innate culture of entrepreneurship that finds business opportunity in tradition. Laxmishanker Pathak, a native Gujarati, arrived in England from Kenya in 1957 with only five pounds in his pocket. His wife Santagaury and he began making authentic Indian food from their kitchen and sold it to their Indian neighbours. In five years, they had acquired a factory. Their award-winning cooking sauces, curry pastes, chutneys, pickles and pappadums are now distributed to more than 40 countries worldwide, including the UK, Europe, Japan, Australia, New Zealand, the United States and Canada. Their customers are no longer just Indians: Patak's has grown to become an internationally successful brand. What is the essential ingredient in these condiments? Spices, which the west has always treasured.

Villages and old towns across Asia are redeveloping and turning themselves into tourist attractions. In China, Zhouzhuang, Xitang and Fengjing, small watertowns near Shanghai, are very good examples. Crisscrossed by canals, with their narrow lanes and old architecture, these towns are great daytrips for those visiting the big city, offering a chance to taste the local cuisine, laze on a boat and guzzle local beer or rice wine.

Chokhi Dhani, a recreated village resort just outside the city of Jaipur in Rajasthan, India, attracts visitors by offering a taste of authentic Rajput food (which you must eat sitting on the floor with your fingers) and hospitality. It is a favourite among conference attendees in Jaipur. Bhaktapur, a Unesco heritage city an hour away from Kathmandu, and Lijiang, yet another Unesco heritage city in China's Yunnan province are profiting from preserving their past, as are Kampung Morten, Melaka and Clan Jetties, Penang (both in Malaysia). The locals have a stake everywhere, selling everything from their handicrafts, to culinary and performing arts to local knowledge. On a grander scale, Aman Nath and Francis Wacziarg are two entrepreneurs who are buying up abandoned, derelict palaces, hunting lodges and havelis (the homes of erstwhile princes and landlords) across India and converting them into five-star properties, striving to keep them authentic by painstakingly unearthing the old designs. Neemrana Hotels (named after the first palace in Rajasthan that they renovated) is now a prestigious brand that is highly differentiated in the hotel business in India. Similarly, when Beijings' hutongs were being demolished in the pre-Olympic cleanup, some home owners decided to renovate their courtyard homes and turn them into uniquely designed homestay experiences. Now, those properties are booked out months in advance.

By using a range of strategies such as craftsmanship and culinary skills, entrepreneurs in Asia are showing that they are indeed profiting through creativity.

Humour

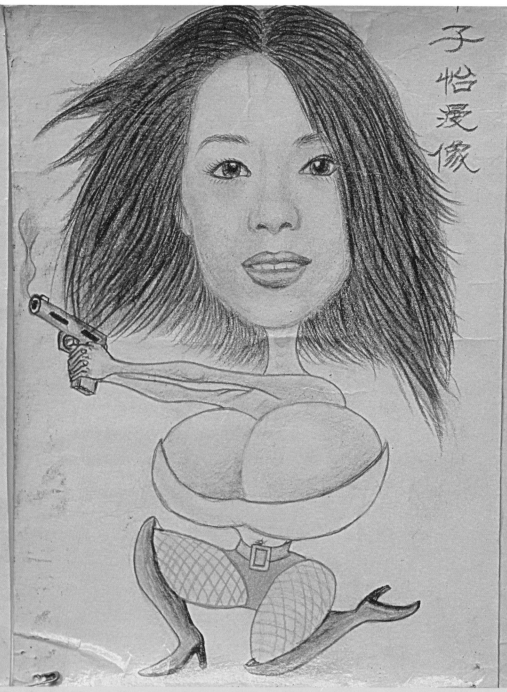

Typified by the nerdy Indian Asok in Dilbert, the comic strip, and Abercrombie & Fitch's T-Shirt series that had slogans like "Wong Brothers Laundry Service - Two Wongs can make it White", Asians are often at the receiving end of many Western jokes.

奥巴马漫像

Going by the depiction of Barack Obama, it seems that they are striking back. Caricatures of Western business leaders such as Bill Gates, as well as popular Asian figures like Zhang Ziyi, abound as commercial artifacts.

They're also learning to laugh at themselves. Tantra is a line of T-Shirts founded by microbiologist turned copywriter turned businessman Ranjiv Ramchandani in India. Tantra enjoys a cult following among young trendy Indians, and now retails in Europe, the Middle-East and Oceania. Tantra's humour draws upon topical events, such as the never-coming-to-fruition plans for the Mumbai metro, Indian rituals such as giving clothes to the washerman *dhobi* (the only other man the lady of the house takes out her clothes for), and uncivil behaviour like pissing in public.

In the Phillippines, the US Armed Forces have quite a presence. One barber decides to have fun by christening his salon 'Hair Force One'.

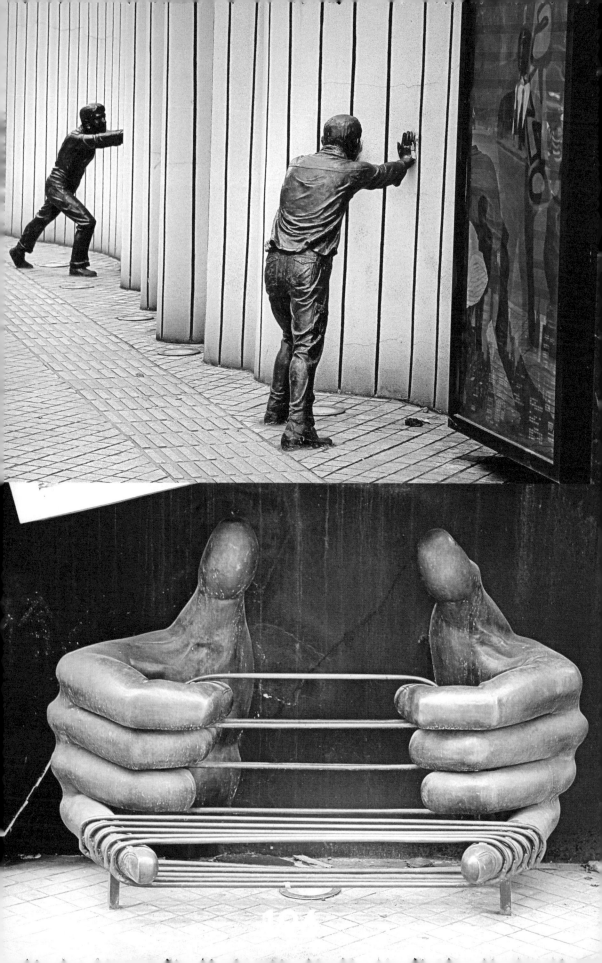

There's humour in public installations in Chengdu, where a wall appears to be held up by two men and another seemingly a jigsaw puzzle with its last piece being put in place. A seat which is crafted to look like a pair of hands playing with rubberbands cannot but elicit a smile from passersby.

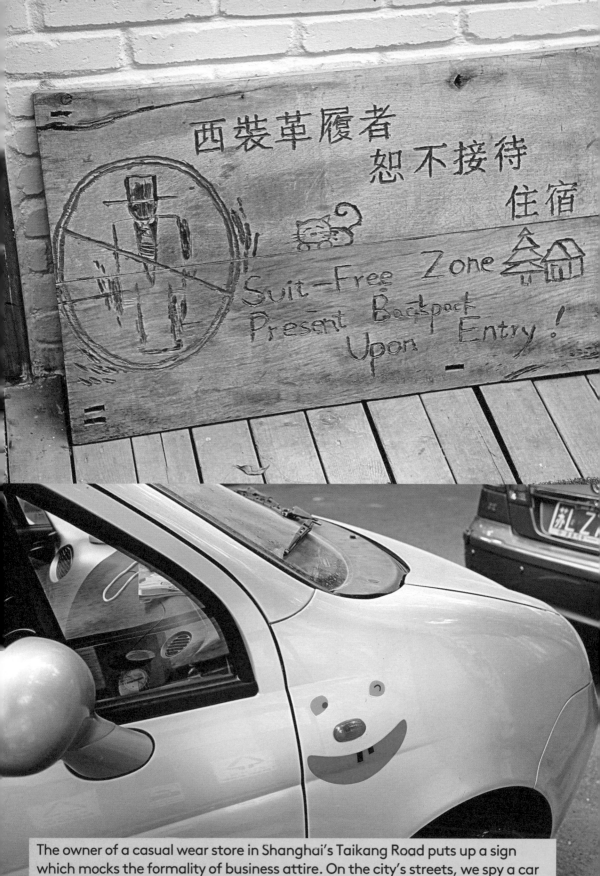

西裝革履者
恕不接待
住宿

Suit-Free Zone
Present Backpack
Upon Entry!

The owner of a casual wear store in Shanghai's Taikang Road puts up a sign which mocks the formality of business attire. On the city's streets, we spy a car whose owner sticks decals which suggest that his car is smiling.

There's irony in a No-Smoking sign at a Delhi cigarette store, and also in the image of worker ants on the back of a removals van on a Tokyo street.

For many Asians, humour is a strategy that alleviates everyday tedium. It allows them to rise above poverty and have fun at the expense of authorities or the establishment. But it also allows us to laugh at ourselves. From time immemorial, morals and values have been communicated through humour.

R.K. Laxman's cartoons have appeared on the front page of The Times of India for 50 years. His 'common man' has expressed frustration with politicians and poked fun at middle-class morality. His humour is directed at the vast human drama - from bickering among super powers, terrorism, corruption in high places, to the immediate problems of pot holes and power shortage, water crisis, soaring prices, strikes, obsession with security and traffic jams, and sometimes even marketing and advertising. Beyond eliciting that daily chuckle, the cartoons always make the everyday reader, the bureaucrat and the politician pause and think, if only for a moment. In many ways, Laxman is playing the role that state jesters such as Birbal and Tenali Rama played in the courts of erstwhile Indian kings centuries ago, pointing out their monarch's follies. The morals and lessons of their tales remain as relevant in contemporary times as they did before, which provides good reason for comic-book publisher Amar Chitra Katha to continue to publish them today, and make them available online for the young digerati in India.

In China, satire and comedy is usually enacted online or in the teahouses in its cities. When Guo Degang performs in a teahouse near Tiananmen Square, tickets always sell out fast. Thirty-three-year-old Guo is not a pop or movie star but a performer of Xiangsheng, or crosstalk, a traditional form of Chinese humour. "He is a man who perfectly mingles traditional crosstalk with modern life features," comments playwright Huang Jisu. Guo is noted for his ability to add modern material to traditional pieces. His crosstalk draws upon every aspect of daily life, from the No. 300 bus to noodles with soybean paste. Fans turn his crosstalk pieces into audio files for download. Do you see any advertising in China featuring crosstalk? Never. Because most managers believe that building brands is serious business.

Those that are brave reap the rewards. Two university students from Guangzhou became immensely popular a few years ago when they recorded a lipsynced version of the Backstreet Boys' hit 'As long as you love me' and posted it on YouTube. Their trademark facial expressions had internet surfers in splits. When a 'regular' TV campaign did not move market shares much, Ogilvy convinced the managers at Motorola to sign them on, because they represent the new face of comedic expression in China. The Backdorm Boys goofy online antics, in which the mobile phone played a role, charmed China's youth and reversed the fortunes of the brand in just two months.

Cartoon

Has Asia had enough of Mickey Mouse? While that might be a difficult question to answer, there is no doubt that local homegrown characters are emerging everywhere. Japan, of course, has been a leader, with Hello Kitty perhaps the most ubiquitous character of all. In 2008, the Japanese government – those somber men in dark suits – appointed the feline as the nation's official tourism ambassador to China and made her part of the Visit Japan campaign. That year, another cat, Doraemon, was anointed Japan's first anime cultural ambassador.

But Japan discovered the value of cartoons and animation many years late. It was even earlier, in 1946 that Bobby Kooka, Air India's commercial director, and art director Umesh Rao created the Maharajah, a royal character who epitomised Indian hospitality. While the airline itself has now jettisoned the Maharajah in favour of 'more contemporary graphics', he lives on in the hearts of people, on restaurant doorways and on the sides of cold water dispensers on India's streets.

The Amul girl, a chubby mascot for India's most popular butter brand, made her appearance on packaging and billboards in 1967, making comments on social problems, and celebrating individual and the nation's achievements alike. For example, when the newly-wedded wife of a reality show contestant was battered, the Amul girl immediately came up with a cheeky rejoinder.

tered, not battered!

Amul
Better halved

While these are the more successful and widespread cartoon characters that pervade Asia's landscape, along with the supremely popular *manga* comics, hundreds of entrepreneurs are creating their own characters, in all shapes and sizes, sometimes irreverent, sometimes dominant, sometimes plain tacky.

チョット お茶 チョット遊ぶ

Fun for Life
P-KUN STATION!

ピーくん P-KU STATION
ステーション

話題の コーナー

イチパチ
1YEN PACHINKO

¥.1 いちぱち
1YEN PACHINKO

209

These characters draw from each other as they mutate across geographies from Pokemon to Papimon and Agumon.

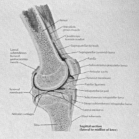

On other occasions, they may take over a whole city, as did the Shanghai Expo mascot *Haibao* for over a year. Or even a whole country, as did the Beijing Olympic mascots, the *Fuwa*. But it is when we see a hospital advertise its services using animation, that's when we believe that this has got be taken seriously!

Forming and signalling identity

The competitive environment Asians live in makes a unique identity a major factor in drawing attention for individuals and small businesses alike. As exposure to different cultures and sub-cultures multiplies, it leads to the general re-evaluation of cultural identity. Individuals form this identity through a creative process of negotiation, not a blind adoption or copying of 'desirable role models'. This cross cultural exchange may sometimes alter and disrupt each society it touches, but it also supports innovation and creative human energies.

警察官
立寄所

THE
PLACE
POLICE
MEN
PATROL

The Japanese *otaku* youth subculture, inspired by anime and mediated by technology, signifies resistance to the rigid hierarchy of traditional society. The *otaku* kids distance themselves from mainstream culture and are obsessed with secret knowledge and subversion.

Senior citizens are renegotiating their identity in a different way. It is part preservation of traditional culture and part exploration of the new. In both instances, it is about a yearning for recognition as a group that is still relevant in modern China, where hundreds of 60 somethings gather in the parks in the morning to dance, sing and do *tai chi* with complete strangers. Let the young go to the gym and block out the sounds of nature with their earphones; we love the fresh air, the touch of another person, and to sing in unison, they say.

The hierarchical nature of most Asian societies lends itself to symbols of showing allegiance to figures of power. One of the most striking examples of this is the act of wearing yellow shirts and red shirts in Thailand. The red shirts are supporters of the exiled leader of the 'masses' Thaksin Shinawatra; while the yellow shirt, traditionally a sign of showing allegiance to the King, is now a symbol of support for the ruling elite. The recent conflict has resulted in more subtle expressions of loyalty, such as pasting stickers on motorcycles.

The hundreds of motorcycle taxi-drivers on Bangkok's streets, on the other hand, wear their *seua win* – zipped, sleeveless, numbered jackets, as a way of signalling the gang they belong to. Each driver must pay protection money to the mafia that controls them and getting a jacket costs 4,000 baht upwards.

So what does an ordinary citizen do with his or her motorcycle? Luxury brand accoutrements – like faux Burberry or Louis Vuitton seat covers - are as much a fashion statement as recognition of the practical necessity of being able to spot your bike amongst the hundreds parked.

These symbols are important because they provide people a creative opportunity. Keeping a pet poodle is symbolic of this middle-aged woman's upper class aspiration, but it is in dyeing the helpless dog that she makes sure that everyone in Chengdu notices her.

Some of this identity is transitory. While on holiday, the desire for experimentation and freedom from social constraints leads many travellers to don beads and faux dreadlocks, everywhere from Goa to Pattaya.

Even as these modern manifestations of identity emerge, there are those who hark back to tradition. There is resurgence in traditional tattoo motifs, as can be seen on the back of this young man in Thailand.

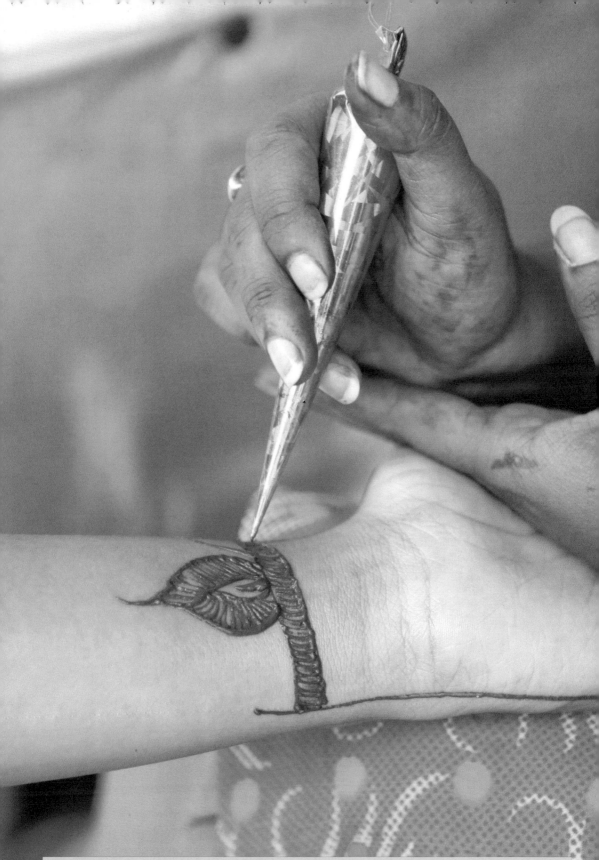

For countless young women across India, festivals and weddings are occasions to get intricate henna patterns drawn on their hands.

What these markers of identity suggest is that Asian individualism needs peer approval. Most individuals see themselves in relation to others. So, it is perfectly fine to go against the grain; and equally acceptable to hold on to certain values in the face of enormous change, so as long as there are enough supporters for your belief.

One such mass, yet highly individual form of expression can be seen in this array of bollards in a Kolkata park. The local civic authorities put up these wooden pillars and encourage local artists and youth to interpret them into imaginary figures.

227

Attention grabbing shop signs

If businesses have to stand out and be noticed amidst the chaos and color on Asia's streets, they must do so visually and viscerally. A shop sign has to do more than merely announce what kind of merchandise lies inside. It must make the pedestrian stop in their tracks or make the passing motorist take a mental note to return on foot.

Using interesting typography, design, colour, natural and recycled materials, sometimes using wordplay and on others characters, the shop signs on the next few pages do just that.

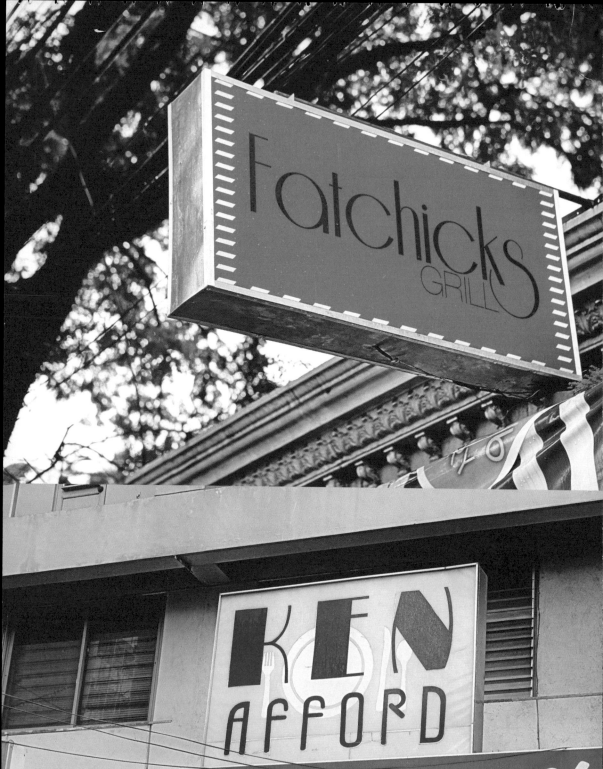

SCENT
— of a —
WOMAN
coffee & food & pub

急 招
收银员、服务员
有经验者优先
待遇店内详询
听雨

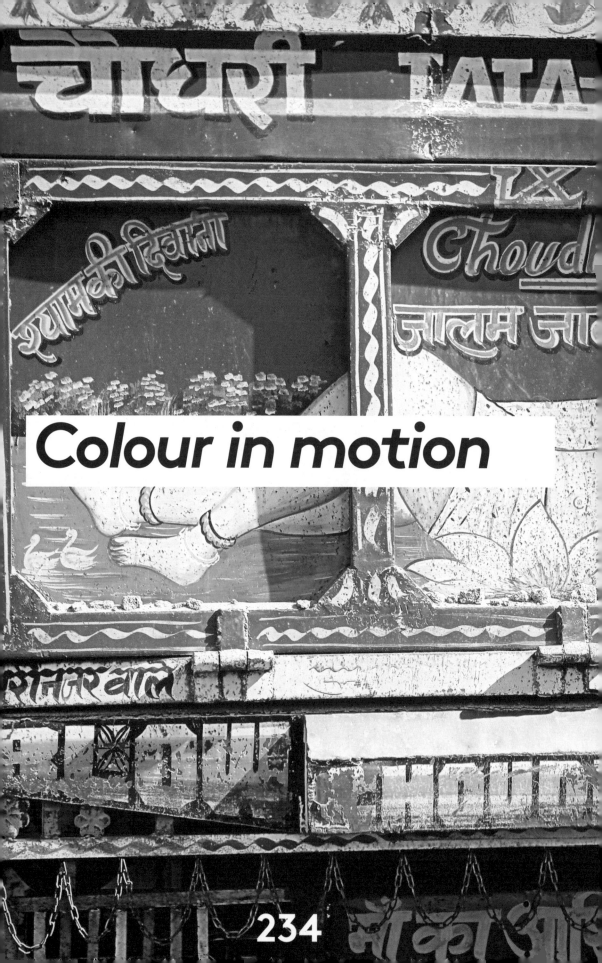

Colour in motion

Perhaps one of the better documented manifestations of Asian creativity is the phenomenon of art-on-wheels. From Pakistani and Indian truck art, to Japanese *Deco-tora*, to Filipino jeepney art, these extravagant designs have served to differentiate these vehicles, signify ownership and imbue them with religious, commercial and cultural meaning.

237

238

Craftsmanship

Even as technology invades every domain of the creative endeavour, in many parts of Asia, people rely on their hands rather than the machine. Painstakingly crafting objects of great beauty as they have done for generations, they wield the chisel, the needle, the hammer and the scissors, and what they come up with graces everything from homes to temples, the human body to the divine.

The skill is learned early, on the potter's wheel in Chengdu. It stays for a lifetime, and is passed down from one generation to another.

The old man carving a printer's block in a saree workshop in Jaipur has a dozen teenage apprentices, just as his own children learned the intricate art from him.

The idolmakers of Kumartuli, near Kolkata, who labour over the clay images of Goddess Durga for months do not leave anything to chance. They transport the idols to the *pandals* themselves – the intensity on their faces and the sinews on their forearms are only matched by those on the demon Mahishasura's image. Should any cracks appear, they repair and repaint on the spot.

It is a succession of craftsmen that ensures that every *saree* woven on the looms in Bengal (or Tamil Nadu, or anywhere else in India for that matter) is a masterpiece. Every bolt of cotton is dyed by hand, set out in the sun to bake and dry, before it is turned into thread. A master weaver then figures out the warp and the weft on his loom, mixing yarns – silk, cotton, even gold and silver thread – and then spends days, sometimes weeks, creating the five yards that will grace the body of an Indian woman.

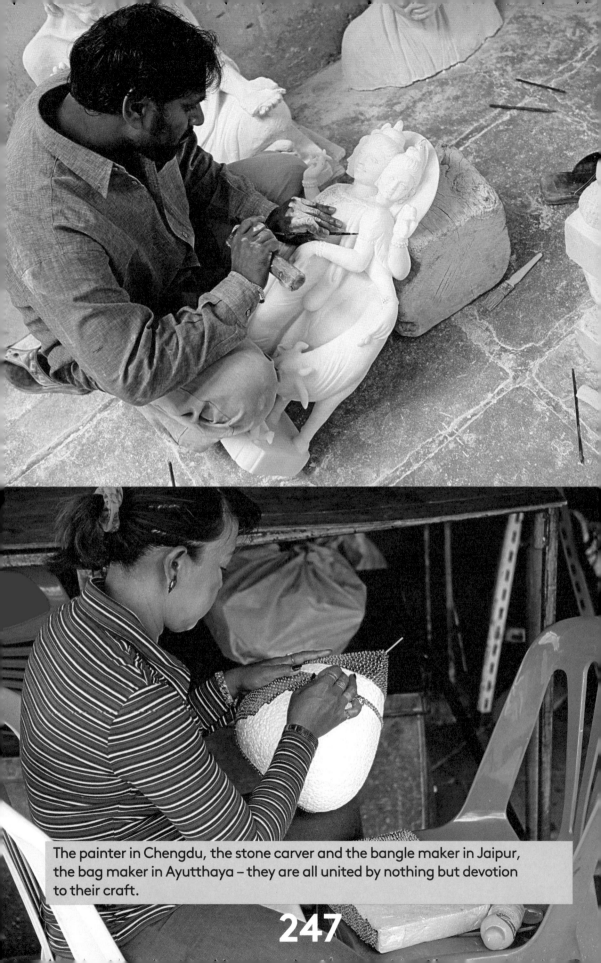

The painter in Chengdu, the stone carver and the bangle maker in Jaipur, the bag maker in Ayutthaya – they are all united by nothing but devotion to their craft.

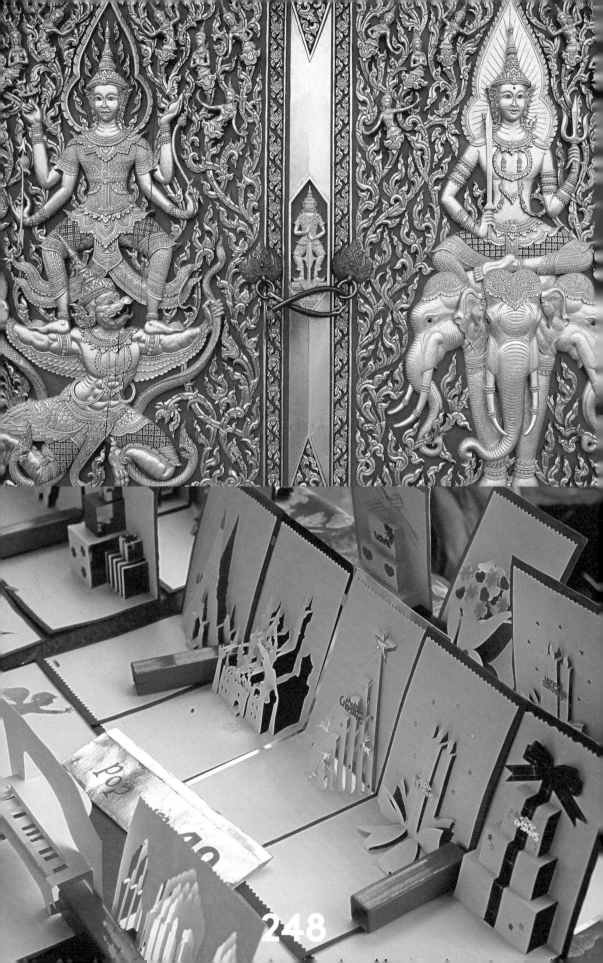

Such devotion gives birth to stunning creations such as the temple panel in Ayutthaya, pop-up papercut greeting cards and colourful bangles in Shanghai, an embroidered and a festooned tree in Chengdu.

It animates reed coin purses and Madhubani paintings in Delhi's crafts bazaar Dilli Haat, and blown glass decorative pieces in Manila. It turns glass sculptors such as Jiang Jiamei from Dalian in China's northeast into minor celebrities.

Loathe to throw away used objects into the garbage bin, eager to stretch their resources to the maximum, many low-income Asians find the most ingenious uses of trash. In Delhi, an auto mechanic recycles a mineral water bottle as an oil dispenser, and another plastic bottle finds a new lease of life as a funnel in Kolkata.

vodafone

यहाँ उपलब्ध है

One jeep driver in Jaipur lashes a discarded election banner on to his vehicle frame to protect his passengers from the sun, and rivets part of a Vodafone sign to protect his tyres from mud. The words 'Vodafone available here' are a delightful irony.

Soft drink and beer brands become the object of many a recycling effort by opportunists. In Bangkok, they turn cans and bottles into hats and bags. One Ayutthaya designer fashions clocks out of soda cans.

Other environmental crusaders pile their recycled artifacts into makeshift mobile shops – a van or a trishaw – and encourage others to turn their trash into cash. At Dilli Haat, a student cycles in every day to sell handmade notebooks.

ขอเชิญ ร่วมบริจาคฝากระป๋อง กับ เป๊ปซี่ กรีน

เพื่อนำไปเป็นวัสดุในการทำขาเทียมให้กับผู้พิการ
มูลนิธิขาเทียม ในสมเด็จพระศรีนครินทราบรมราชชนนี
เพื่อลดปริมาณขยะและภาวะโลกร้อน!!

The companies who generate the waste in the first place are taking note, and they have launched highly visible, public trash collecting and recycling programs. A recycling sign made out of bottle caps – that's a good start!

Fusion

Arata Isozaki is a Japanese architect whose work has sometimes been described as 'schizophrenic eclectic'. He says, "I can't be Japanese and I can't be Western – but I can understand both. I am double binded – but, and this is perhaps most important – I am also in a position that generates a great deal of energy and creativity." With greater exposure, an ever-growing number of individuals and businesses across Asia are experiencing this double-bindedness.

For all its symbolism as the great American brand, Starbucks has tried hard (and succeeded) in blending into the urban landscape in China and Korea. Under the carved wooden eaves of a traditional oriental marketplace like Shanghai's Yu Garden, they serve the rice dumpling *Zongzi* during the Dragon Boat Festival, apart from the regular cappuccino.

The same principles are applied in Seoul and Chengdu.

스타벅스커피

일반음식점

The most successful fast food chain in China, Kentucky Fried Chicken (KFC) goes even further by introducing to its menu something that is Chinese every month: rice congee, stir-fried vegetables, chicken that is grilled rather than fried (the Chinese believe that grilling is less 'heaty'). At the same Yu Garden, one of the KFC outlets has a stone lion guarding its gates.

It isn't surprising, then, when political pop artists like Wang Guangyi slap KFC's logo on Cultural Revolution imagery in their posters. It is such incongruity that makes the designs appealing.

McDonald's is catching up. Across Thailand, Ronald McDonald welcomes customers with folded hands, as if saying *Sawasdee*. And in a delightful reversal, a local streetside restaurant has appropriated the restaurant's icon, but is shown waving.

At a souvenir stall in Qibao, a water-town near Shanghai, a group of young women – all clad in western clothes – seek to fuse their identity when they don imperial costume and have their pictures taken.

In Shanghai's art district Moganshan Road, Israeli artist and former Shanghai resident Basmat Levin presents a solo show of work inspired by Tang Dynasty figures and scenes. She appropriates Facebook as a title for her show featuring intricately detailed oil portraits of Eastern and Western characters.

Carol's Cafe in Shanghai's Taikang Road, a fashionable warren of boutiques, cafes and art galleries, proclaims it in its signage. But it is on Carol's tables that the combination of a western setting and tableware, designed using traditional Chinese motifs that the effect of that fusion comes alive.

On other occasions, it is sheer fascination of some things Western which gives rise to creative incongruity. The Buddhist monk in charge of the construction of Wat Pariwat, a temple in Bangkok, was a fan of David Beckham. So he had Beckham's crouching figure carved into the altar and covered in gold leaf.

273

274

Urbanisation and the role of creativity

-Urban centres have always been cauldrons of creativity. In the emerging world, cities have greater economic and creative flexibility to attract talent and business. In Asia, cities like Singapore, Bangalore, Beijing and Shanghai, as cited by Richard Florida in The Flight of the Creative Class, leveraged investments in the development and retention of homegrown talent to reverse the historic brain drain and reattract those who had left in search of better opportunity. Now, these centres draw in talented people from across geographies and cultures. Add Bandung, Dalian, Manila and Chengdu to that list. As these cities become more vibrant and globally-oriented places, their traditional attitudes towards tolerance and diversity change, and, as a result, artistic and cultural amenities take root.

276

Municipal authorities act as catalysts in the transformation of the city. Chengdu's Wide Lane and Narrow Lane, once home to Manchu officials and Manchu soldiers, fell into disrepair and stayed that way for decades until the local authorities restored the entire area. The modern cafes, guest-houses and boutiques of this 17th century precinct nestle against city-sponsored murals reminding visitors of an ancient way of life.

The canvas available to city governments can be immense, and all it takes is a bit of bravery to imbue urban landscapes with colour. Who says that the space under flyovers and along subways needs to be boring? In Jaipur, the pillars are encased in giant vinyl wraps depicting the city's old landmarks; in Tokyo, a similar space is turned into an exhibit for emerging artists.

One part of a wall in Shanghai's Moganshan Road is painted to resemble a hut out of a fairytale. In Yu Garden, a poster shows how the street looked a century ago.

A mural in Seoul is made up of thousands of small photographs taken by those who entered a photography competition. It provides a vivid demonstration of the citizens' individual expression assembled into a collective feeling of participation.

Qibao old town, near Shanghai, features an entire building with a giant fresco of cascading waterfalls and pavilions, even as a real pavilion and rockery abut the scenery. The rear of a temporary display booth in Yu Garden joins together three very different eras of Shanghai history – Chinese, colonial, and ultramodern. The cutout images of seagulls in that installation seem to represent the citizens of Shanghai, as they swoop effortlessly from one to the other.

Even park and roadside benches are being turned into objets d'art. In Manila, the sculpture of a man reading a newspaper; in Chengdu, a series of park benches with images of a young man, a young woman, and Cupid.

285

Precincts often compete amongst each other to draw residents and visitors alike, by doing up their environs in colour, as can be seen in the Yunnan Food Street in Shanghai. Lanterns, animal figures and floral decorations, all provide an opportunity for local craftspeople to showcase their talent.

But even cities need to remind themselves of nature. While parks are an obvious form of breaking the endless stream of concrete, creating displays out of shrubbery – as can be seen in the musician figures of Seoul, and *Haibao*, the Shanghai Expo mascot – are another way to bring green into the urban centre.

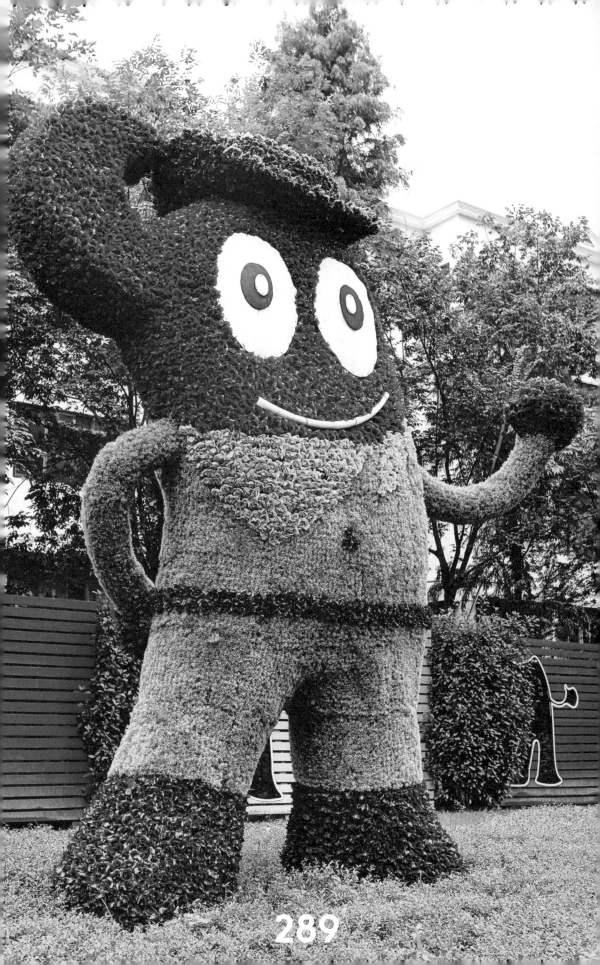

289

Nature is brought in through artwork as well. Be it the sculpture of apples in a Shanghai park, on which perches a seemingly greedy crow, or a concrete pillar in a Seoul mall which suddenly sprouts branches when it reaches the ceiling, natural imagery works its way into even the most densely populated regions.

แยกนี้เกิดอุบัติเห
ขับรถโปรดระมัด
สน

PHYATHA
HOSPITAL
โรงพยาบาลพญา

Call Center 17

Human nature is all too evident in most big cities, and law enforcers across Asia's cities are beginning to feel the need to take a somewhat creative route to keep citizens in line. Since they, like most cities do not have enough policemen to mind the traffic, the Bangkok Police came up with the idea of installing lifelike mannequins to deter speeding drivers, especially at night.

The Metro Manila Development Authority (MMDA) painted the sidewalks of some of the city's thoroughfares with pink lines. These pink lines set off the pedestrians' rightful walking space.

In Kolkata, the police department waxes poetic, when it draws a parallel between the stripes on a prisoner's uniform and those on a zebra crossing, creatively reminding speeding drivers of the possible consequences they face. The Bangkok police department believes in poetry, or at least doggerel. They help tourists to recognise the real policemen (as opposed to private security guards) by saying 'Meet our Men in Brown, We know this Town'.

เหตุด่วน เหตุร้าย แจ้ง **191**
ดับเพลิง แจ้ง **199**
สนับสนุนโดย

AIA

Some police booths are being designed rather interestingly, perhaps enabled by corporate sponsorship. The one with a helmet in Manila does look striking, as does a purple fire truck in Manila, emblazoned with flames.

If the fire department and the police department can embrace such vivid colour and style, why should the power department feel left behind? In Ayutthaya, they're allowing the transformer boxes to be painted over with scenes of enforcing discipline in school, and preserving nature. Did we say anything about politicians being colourful and creative? That would need another book. For the moment, let's move on to explore how businesses are profiting from creativity.

The business value of creativity

The size of the Indian film industry, not counting piracy, has been estimated by industry insiders at USD 2 billion. In 2009, USD 3.1 billion worth of Chinese art was sold at auctions. But those are the big players. Small entrepreneurs across Asia have monetised their creativity for generations.

Jaipur's blue pottery makers such as Kripal Kumbh, Neerja International and Natha Arts produce absolute gems and are cited in Fodor's Guide and Lonely Planet.

Kailash Mehta, proprietor of Moorti Arts in Jaipur, and other idolmakers like her run thriving businesses making and exporting idols of not just Hindu, Jain, Sikh and Christian deities, but also figures of business leaders and historic figures.

For over 40 years, Anokhi's craftspersons have perfected the art of handblock and screen printing of textiles. Their garments and furnishings retail in Jaipur, Mumbai, Kolkata, New Delhi, Chennai and Bangalore are widely exported.

A.L. Paper House is India's largest manufacturer of recycled cotton paper, all of it made by hand for the past four centuries. The colourful gift boxes, bags and wrapping paper made by their artisans were once prized by Indian emperors. Today, the Indian government recognises them as the Best Handmade Paper Company.

Even as the big-name artists in China command astronomical prices for their paintings, small gallery owners in Shanghai, Chengdu and Beijing find enough buyers amongst a growing middle class to keep their businesses ticking along. In Japan, we find artists selling caricatures of Western and Japanese stars and politicians, while in Seoul one-of-a-kind coasters carved out of wood and painted with natural designs, command a premium price.

Asia's gigantic music industry is kept humming melodiously by hundreds of musical instrument makers and stores. Some, like Delhi's Lahore Music House, have become institutions. Founded by the late Sardar Harcharan Singh Sachdeva in Lahore's Anarkali Bazaar more than 50 years ago, the shop moved to Delhi after the partition of India. They offer a range of string, wind and percussion instruments and will ship anywhere in the world.

The shops on Shanghai's Jinling Road play no small role in satiating China's huge appetite for learning and performing music. Shiny showrooms stock Yamaha, Baldwin and the homegrown Pearl River pianos side-by-side with violins, violas and cellos. The traditional Chinese drum shops selling *gugin* and *erhu* are returning to favour as China delves into its musical past. Revenues in the musical instruments industry have been estimated at USD 2.5 billion in 2010.

The wedding industry is even bigger - USD 90 billion big. In 2009, 14 million Chinese got married. When they do, they do it with flourish creativity – from the design of the dress, to the photo album, venue and food styling. No wonder then, that costume design shops abound and set up their displays in pedestrian malls where young people date and shop.

A different kind of togetherness is enabled by Filipino bakery chain Kink Cakes, which calls itself 'rated X-tra different'. With names like 'Prisoner of Love', 'Hot Babe' and 'Viagra Night', their innovative cake designs are inspired by adult humour – ideal gifts for bachelor parties, bridal showers and anniversaries. The innovation extends to ingredients, with marshmallows being used in the icing instead of butter to keep the cakes from melting in the steamy Manila heat. Since the business was founded ten years ago, they have expanded to seven stores.

อบซิตอบ
ก.ก. 150.-

ลูกพรุน
ก.ก. 150.-

บ๊วยกับทิม
ก.ก. 120.-

บ๊วยทฤระ
ก.ก. 150.-

ฝรั่งหยี
ก.ก. 120.-

แอปเปิ้ลอบกรอบ
ก.ก. 120.-

แคลดา รูเซนี
ก.ก. 120.-

ก.ก. 100

Staying with the theme of food, this fruit stall owner in a Bangkok market takes extra care in arranging her merchandise in an interesting pattern, which makes a shopper stop in her tracks and buy.

311

In Chengdu, a local brand of dried beef attracts customers by having a salesman paint his face in the same Sichuan opera style mask that's on their packaging and then stand outside the shop.

Mobility becomes the differentiator for this ATM-on-wheels in Bangkok. At the same time, its bright pink colour clearly signals who the preferred customers are.

All the owner of Burger Machine in Manila has to do is drive into a vacant parking lot, unfold the flaps of his gaily painted vending van, set up the barstools outside his window, and his business is up and running.

During China's Cultural Revolution, farmers from a village 60 kilometres from Shanghai were trained to paint images glorifying peasant life. Thus was born the colourful Jinshan Peasant Painting style. Today, the descendants of those farmers, with the help of the local government, have turned their village into a tourist destination.

315

Unlocking Asia's creative potential

We're sure that, by now, you have recognised the tremendous imagination that Asians possess. You have seen how they put that imagination to use, in their personal lives, to further and strengthen their social norms, and in their business ventures. When all these brave small and medium businesses, and the individuals who run them can profit from creativity, what's holding bigger, more established businesses back? And how can they take advantage of this innate knack for innovation?

TAKE THE ANTI-ELITIST VIEW

The elitist or genius view of creativity, which has been dominant in rhetoric for many decades, holds that creativity is a rare individually-exercised talent, unable to be taught. The differential distribution of power and resources among individuals and groups in society seem to impact the generation of creative ideas. Those that have the most power and resources have the luxury to be the most creative.

All our evidence suggests otherwise. It is often those with the fewest resources who are most creative, simply because they have goals to meet and problems to solve in their daily existence. Creativity is not a luxury to them; it is a survival mechanism. Moreover, creative solutions are not conceived in isolation but are worked out through direct contact with others. Creators work within a social milieu or community and are in touch with the beliefs and ideas of others. Most build on what has already been introduced. The cross-fertilisation of ideas along with thorough problem exploration enables groups that interact perhaps to be more creative than individuals working alone. Improvisation – one of the dominant features of creativity - is a cooperative effort. It builds a sense of community. The creative process has a high tolerance for ambiguity, and the circularity of Asian thinking supports ambiguity.

In Asia, most surviving historical manifestations were initiated and sponsored by royalty. This gives credence to the elitist or genius theory of creativity. From the Taj Mahal and the magnificent forts of India, to the Suzhou Gardens and Ming Dynasty pottery in China, to the Angkor Wat, creative objects were the work of imperial craftspeople. Everyday creativity was neither documented nor preserved. As the monarchies were replaced or run over, the creativity they patronised in these cultures was deemed to have died with them. Which is why, today, we have to immerse ourselves in everyday life to unearth it and take pains to point out the sense of creativity and ideas that underpin daily activity. Such commonplace creativity is the result of a multidirectional relationship between cultural, political and social forces, which creates a need for adaptation and a churn for new ideas. This is even truer in the 21st century, as contact with other cultures multiplies through travel and technology. The social and cultural contexts not only help nurture creativity, they also serve to evaluate and legitimise creative ideas and products. The idea of using a washing machine to churn milk may have occurred to one individual, but it caught on like wildfire among dhaba owners simply because the characteristics of simplicity and resourcefulness underpinned it. It was a shared need, felt in a shared cultural and business context.

The implications for our marketing communications business are profound. As we mentioned in our introduction, many elitist managers continue to harbour the belief that the mass consumer in Asia is incapable of relating to creative, non-linear ideas and expressions. 'Simplify the messages', 'Repeat, emphasize the point/ promise', they say over and over again, attempting to strip nuance and subtlety down to the lowest common denominator. If everyday conversation in Asia is suffused with metaphor and hyperbole, if simple gestures can communicate more than the spoken word, surely the same modes of communication can be applied to a 30 second TV commercial. Those who have stopped underestimating their consumers and their ability to interpret creative messages are indeed benefiting.

Pidilite Industries in India believed that carpenters in India would be able to understand the humour of an overcrowded bus with a Fevicol adhesive sign painted at the back or a fishing rod with drops of the adhesive on it to catch fish. The Coca-Cola Company exhibited bravery when they understood the cleverness and refreshingly different approach of Coach Calorie Buster. That Hong Kong campaign asked people to take a nap, or kiss, to burn the one calorie in a can of Coke Light. In China, when a television commercial shows young people jumping into the desert sand which then transforms into a pool of cool water because they've drunk Sprite, TV viewers don't say "but that's not real, it can't be possible". They relate to the metaphor and think of it as cool (pun intended). As a result, Sprite is the most popular carbonated soft drink in China's second-tier cities. All three brands have benefited enormously from believing in the creative appreciation capability of their everyday consumers.

REVISIT MASLOW'S HIERARCHY

By and large, brands exist (and brand / marketing managers believe) in order to satisfy a need the consumer or prospect has. Since the end of the Second World War, Abraham Maslow's hierarchy of needs has provided a convenient framework to identify the motivations that a brand could address. Taught in all business schools, the reductionist model is wonderfully simple to understand, and everyone can relate to it. It is elegant in PowerPoint™, and often makes a convincing case. It works on the principle of elimination, which can be adopted quickly to give target audience analysis a sharper definition and focus.

But Maslow developed his theory in post-war Poland, which possessed an entirely different set of social and political circumstances from contemporary Asia. We now believe that his theory doesn't work anymore. We are not questioning Maslow's classification of human needs at all. That is very lucid, and offers a convenient classification. What we question is the hierarchical nature of the needs. In the developing and developed societies of 21st century Asia, the hierarchy of needs as posited by Maslow is no longer valid.

Let's consider some of the evidence:

- Physiological needs are supposed to do with the maintenance of the human body and food, health and sleep, and nothing matters till they are met. Significant populations deprive themselves of food in order to enhance their self-esteem (through dieting), or to seek divine blessing and/or be part of a group (through religious fasting or depriving oneself of specific kinds of food – otherwise deemed nutritious - among Hindus and Muslims). The religious mendicants (sadhus) in India take this to an extreme level – being completely self-actualised without having a roof over their heads and no sources of income.

- In our pursuit of success in career and business, or even relationships (to fulfill our need for self-esteem), we are depriving ourselves of another physiological need – sleep. Maslowian theory would argue – to stretch the point a bit – that unless we had a good night's rest, we wouldn't be able to achieve recognition for our work the next day. But when someone comments at the beginning of an important meeting 'looks like you haven't slept last night', it is actually deemed as a compliment – a recognition of the hard work put in. When we stay up late – whether it is partying or studying hard for the exams or making love – and are rewarded for it by the warm glow on our partner's face or an A grade, it is by not satisfying a physiological need that we satisfy a higher order need. A global survey of people's sleeping habits by AC Nielsen says that 40% of people in Asia Pacific are burning the midnight oil, compared with 34% of Americans and 32% Europeans.

- Some South Koreans are casting aside their need for safety, in their pursuit of self-actualisation as they undertake missionary and charity work overseas. They visit countries where their safety is not guaranteed, as the kidnapping of 23 South Koreans by the Taliban in Afghanistan makes clear. South Korea ranks second among the nations whose citizens undertake missionary work abroad, with 16,616 missionaries working in 173 countries.

- The Buddhist monks in Myanmar, assumed to be in a per-petual state of self-actualisation and enlightenment by the ruling military junta, take to the streets because they would like to expand their role in society and because their safety and physiological needs have been denied.

- Starbucks started the trend, admittedly, inspired by the roadside cafes in Italy, of making coffee something that didn't satisfy a physical need but served as social glue. The maid cafes at Akihabara in Japan take the role of the cafe to a new level. Of particular appeal to the Japanese otaku (fans of anime cartoons), they satisfy a somewhat perverse need for female subjugation. The young waitresses wearing maid uniforms treat their otaku customers as masters. The cafe, then, meets their need for self-esteem. It is a rather unique need that a business strives to fulfill.

- In community-oriented Asian cultures, the need for social belongingness and respect often takes precedence over the more basic survival needs. Many people spend a lot of money during festivals or in inviting people (sometimes above their social status) home for dinner even though their home needs repair. The ingrained cultural belief of 'Atithi Devo Bhava' (the guest is God) makes them cut corners with their own comfort in order to provide more for guests. Munshi Premchand, a writer and social commentator in India, wrote a poignant take of a family whose only means of protecting its shame was a curtain for the front door made from the saris of the women of the house. Across apartment blocks in Asia (and more keenly felt in the developing nations), families compete fiercely to acquire new consumer durables and to send their children to good, sometimes expensive schools – all done to gain social respect. In the villages of South and Southeast Asia, and mainland China, the same sense of social recognition leads to a greater penetration of TV sets than toilets. In the continent's overcrowded cities, it makes them buy a car before they own an apartment.

In his later adaptation of the five stages, Maslow added two more needs between esteem and self-actualisation: the need to know and understand, which explains the cognitive need of the academic and the need for aesthetic beauty, which he described as the emotional need of the artist. It is the importance of these needs in the lives of Asians everywhere that makes us challenge Maslow's assumptions.

-   We have the evidence that aesthetic beauty is a key strategy that people use to seek love and affection. In that sense, it is not the emotional need of the artist (who is always viewed as a better endowed being, creatively), but the need of every woman who is making herself up or doing up her home. It is the survival need of the small business owner who makes an interesting sign for his business so that it can be differentiated and remembered. It is the tuk-tuk driver's need to belong to a visually expressive group that makes him paint his vehicle so brightly, or the truck driver's need to belong to a verbally expressive group that makes him write very creative couplets on the back of his truck.

-   Look at what's happening with housing. A home is no longer just a place for shelter, no matter how humble it is. Villagers in tribal parts of India imbue their homes with aesthetic beauty, painting designs on their walls. Apartment owners in China's boomtowns decorate them with duplicates of paintings by the Renaissance masters. Homeowners in Thailand create the most colourful gates to their homes. People everywhere are giving their homes a unique dimension that enhances their sense of self-esteem and earns the admiration of others.

-   Learning an art form – dance or music – is a custom that pervades South and East India, and lower middle-class families cut corners to ensure that their daughters (mostly) learn something. Her creative ability serves as a differentiator when she is later being evaluated as a prospective bride. The huge wave to learn western classical music and ballet in China and South Korea stems as much from a desire for prosperity as it does from creative expression. The role of creativity has been pushed down to serving a safety need. If fame is achieved, it comes as a bonus.

With Maslow's hierarchy turned topsy-turvy, brand owners would do well to re-examine the needs that their products and brands fulfil. In dynamic Asia, that role is constantly evolving. Mobile phones, when they were introduced in the mid 1990s, were a status symbol. About 50% of Asia now can't do without one. For itinerant workers and businessmen, it is the essential business tool, allowing the former to find and the latter to do work. For parents of school and college girls, it is a way of trying to ensure their safety. For the migrant, it is how s/he keeps in touch with the family back home. For many young people, it provides entertainment and is a social connector. Motor-scooters go from being a mere mode of transportation on the crowded streets to fuelling a young college girl's individuality and becoming a symbol of independence. A fast food chain is no longer just a place for families or young people to experience new cuisines, but it becomes a place where a village girl realises her dreams by getting employed. And as people become more conscious of the impact of their consumption on nature (a moral need), an oil company stops being the guilty party and takes on the mantle of embracing change in the form of encouraging cleaner fuels.

The travesty in the above examples lies in the fact that companies and brands have only responded to changes in society. If they want to lead the change, they must be brave, and they must embrace a creative mindset to seek unconventional solutions.

RECOGNISE CULTURAL DIVERSITY

The cultural diversity in Asia is both an opportunity and a minefield for managers in transnational corporations. As Asians modernise across every region, brands and their communications seem on the surface to serve as an engine for modernity, progress and cultural homogenisation. Samsung, Nokia, McDonald's, Adidas, Nike and Coke signs can be seen all across the diverse landscape. But do they mean the same thing to all people everywhere? And what role does creativity play in either creating a new brand culture or in assimilating within an existing one?

Food offers a very good barometer of the degree of cultural diversity within a nation, or, indeed, a city. The greater the available options, the more open the society. Tastes are cultivated over generations, indeed, centuries, and for food brands, customisation is a necessity, not a nice-to-have.

Maggi noodles, that money-spinner from Nestlé, is a great example of a brand that first created a new culture and then expanded its influence by assimilating within local cultures. In the 1980s, as a new generation of educated mothers began to raise children, breaking away from traditional norms as the joint-family system eroded, they realised that they had to make food more interesting for their kids. Up until then, noodles were only eaten out at so-called Chinese restaurants, and were invariably a treat. When Maggi introduced the 'two-minute noodles', they knew that they not only had to make it easy for mothers to make, but it also had to be appetising enough for kids to wolf down. The brand communications then showed kids arriving home from school hungry, the mother surprising them with noodles, and the kids slurping it all up. To alleviate her fears of the food being nutritious, and to get her a bit more involved in the act of cooking, the ads and the pack itself suggested garnishing with carrots, peas and other such good things. It did not take very long for Maggi noodles to become the Indian child's favourite snack. A new taste had been introduced, a new food culture born, and to a society that was just modernising, it was a symbol of modernity.

Yet, pockets of resistance remained. That's where Nestlé's embracing of the local culture helped them. Rather than insist on the purity of the original recipe, they added a whole range of flavours that were based on regional spices – sambaar flavour for example – and even the resistant pockets gave in. Maggi's current portfolio in India, which spans from soups to pizza toppings to sauces (in tamarind, mint, coriander and chili flavours, too) to noodles made from rice, wheat and pulses, is about as diverse as the spices in the cosmopolitan Indian housewife's larder. It is something that the brand's owners in Vevey wouldn't have dreamed of 30 years ago. Then the norm was selling one standard Nescafé instant coffee in India for decades. Several fast-food chains have taken the cue. Pizza outlets offer tandoori chicken toppings in the north, and chettinad chicken in the south. McDonald's offers vegetarian burgers in every restaurant in India, in deference to a large population that does not eat meat. Not a single McDonald's outlet in India serves the staple beef hamburger.

The food courts of Singapore, that most intercultural, interracial city in Asia, are a testament to cultural diversity. As Shanghai and Beijing become homes to a growing population of expatriates and Chinese from other parts of the country, their restaurants offer 78 international cuisines, including Cuban, Irish and Nepalese, and 11 different kinds of cuisine from China's different regions. Kentucky Fried Chicken restaurants offer rice congee, crab claws and fried dough on their menu, along with a host of Chinese-inspired chicken recipes. Haagen Dazs and Starbucks serve up green tea- flavoured ice cream and coffee respectively. In India, a quirky practice of spiking one's cola with a dash of lemon juice motivated Pepsi to introduce a lemon-flavoured cola. Playing around with recipes is a risky affair – you never know if customers would like the fusion, or would they hark back to authenticity. So far, both seem to be working for the food and beverage business.

AMPLIFY, OR SMOOTHEN THE CULTURAL TENSION

To the person on the street, as much as to the creative person in an agency, cross-cultural banter and tension is fertile ground for new ideas. Which brings us to the case of Samsung riding on a recent trend – that of South Korea being a successful exporter of culture, popularly called the 'Korean wave'. Through its popular entertainment products, South Korean culture is gaining recognition and acceptance among consumers in Asia, thus leading to tourism and opening the door for South Korean products and services. Combining great design and price with advertising campaigns featuring South Korean superstars, Samsung now boasts larger market share than Sony in China. Interestingly still, this 'Korean Wave' has a side-effect beyond consumer electronics: it is helping shape the Chinese woman's notions of beauty. Rather than adopt cosmetic and fashion trends directly from the west, they allow trends to be interpreted by the Koreans (and the Japanese), figure out if the styles and colour are suitable for the Oriental complexion and body, and then embrace it.

Accentuating a culture's traits can provide a point of drama – as did a series of TV commercials for Coca Cola, featuring the actor Aamir Khan as a Bihari, Bengali and Nepali, in India a few years ago. The well known Canadian-born actor Mark Roswell, known across China as Dashan, provides similar comic or dramatic counterpoints on Chinese television.

Sometimes a local culture gets obscured in relentless pressure from globalised brands. It was during the late 1980s that a remarkable thing happened in Thailand. Before that time, Bangkok's advertising industry took cues from hard-selling Madison Avenue. All that changed with a bottle of beer and an Australian adman at Ogilvy & Mather. "The first thing Barry Owen saw in Thailand was a country of greenery, of water," recalls Bhanu Inkawat of Leo Burnett of the now-retired Ogilvy guru. "He started using it in the Singha beer commercial, which has become a classic campaign. He gave back to Thais the Thai aspect. To see it through Thai, not Western, eyes." The 1989 TV commercial for the brew, marketed as Singha in some countries, featured arresting scenery tied together by the theme of conservation - both previously unseen in local ads. Owen's creative spark ignited nothing less than a revolution in the then-moribund Thai ad industry. Thai creators began focusing on goods and customers to devise campaigns that made products part of people's lives in ways not distorted by foreign artifice. The creative awards which filmmakers like Creative Juice/G1 win so regularly is the outcome of that pioneering spirit.

The Indian advertising industry went through a similar trans-formation, but it came from within. With a heritage that extended back to the early 20th century, most Indian writers were trained in the British tradition. They grew up working on brands like Horlicks, Ovaltine and Lux, and both thought and wrote in English. Or so they did until Piyush Pandey changed everything in the 1990s. As the reach of television expanded, so did the value of communicating in the local language and idiom. Piyush's hallmark work at Ogilvy in India, for brands such as Cadbury, Fevicol and Asian Paints infused the market with a sense of cultural identity that people found relatable and heartwarming. Twenty years on, that identity remains strong. Says Piyush: "Every society has its own signs and symbols of identification and they never lose their relevance. There is no denying the fact that a group of consumers has become more global in its affections, but a much bigger section is still very much rooted in its Indianness."

For many companies, globalisation is a fait accompli in business. The future success and survival of companies will depend on the ability of their management to understand and motivate both a culturally diverse workforce and consumer base. They will need to go beyond oversimplified assumptions of the 'East' to allow different perspectives of creativity to be voiced. They must begin noting nuances and have the confidence to design products and marketing programmes that are based not on global templates, but on locally relevant perception.

Thirty years ago, thinking strategically about business was revolutionary. It allowed visionaries to shape value creation in entirely new ways. The result was the death of conglomerates and the birth of the modern transnational. Today, the average trans-national corporation is packed to the gills with strategists. The language, vocabulary, and ideas of strategic thinking per-meate it.

But that also means that everyone and their grandmother knows how to pick profitable markets, segment them, price goods and services, analyse competitors, understand industry economics, and so on.

Strategy itself, in a very real sense, is becoming a commodity. In a world where strategy is a commodity, creativity becomes the vital factor from which value flows. When everyone can think strategically about everything, the locus of value creation shifts from out-thinking everyone to out-creating them.

And that requires a recognition that creativity is indeed pervasive.

FOOTNOTES

1   Seitz, Jay A. (2003) *The Political Economy of Creativity*.
     Creativity Research Journal. Vol. 15, No. 4, 385-392
2   Maeda, Matabee Kenji (2001): *Creativity from Adversity – Three
     Breakthroughs at Maeda Corporation*. Center for Quality of Management
     Journal. Volume 10, Number 2. Cambridge, MA.
3   Quoted in Maira, Shakti. *A Vision for our Arts*. The Hindu, Sunday Magazine
     supplement. April 2, 2006. Chennai, India
4   Cornwell-Smith, Philip: *Very Thai*. River Books, Bangkok. July 2005. Page 11.
5   Piracy causes $1 billion loss to Indian entertainment industry.
     The Times of India, August 21, 2010
6   Wang Bo, *Putting the ink on a deal takes a new meaning*.
     China Daily, May 17 2010

ACKNOWLEDGMENTS

Raw has been long in the making. But as its 'makers', we have protected it fiercely from the managers, preferring it to be shaped by the voices on the street. Yet, there are several people we must thank for being our partners on this long journey:

Paul Matheson, co-creator of the idea.

Godfathers **Miles Young, Tham Khai Meng, Tim Isaac** and **Paul Heath**. Tim Isaac for his proofreading.

Sarah Maclean, who almost saw it through to the end, before handing over to **Nayumi Nagase** and **Marcus Jilla**, who did.

Our wonderful father-son photographer duo, **Thomas** and **Steffen Billhardt**. People will buy this book because of your photos, not our text. We wish they'd read our text, too.

Albert Leeflang, our superb designer, who gave form to our collection of text and images.

Alvin Chin, who helped make all of this a reality.

Grace Yong, who stood by and supported us all.

Jeremy Katz, incisive, superbly helpful editor as ever.

John Midgley and **Catharine Snow**, who believed that this was a project worth shepherding to the bookshelves.

Our families, who wondered if this project was real or fiction, for over four years.

Kunal Sinha and David Mayo

Local knowledge and insights are key to getting under the skin of a city - thank you to our dedicated team of local experts who guided us through the cities they call home:

Amorntat Soonthornsawad / Ogilvy Bangkok, **'Jo' Teerasut Kayourapan** / Ogilvy Bangkok, **Bubbly Encarnacion** / Ogilvy Makati City, **Jane Ling** / Ogilvy Shanghai, **Melissa Parsey** / formerly Ogilvy Shanghai, **Serena Park** / Ogilvy Seoul, **Azusa Fukai** / Ogilvy Tokyo, **Gavin MacDonald** / formerly Ogilvy Singapore, **Rahul Khurana** / Ogilvy Delhi.

AUTHOR & PHOTOGRAPHER
KUNAL SINHA

Kunal Sinha is Regional Cultural Insights Director, Ogilvy & Mather Asia/Pacific, and Chief Knowledge Officer, China based in Shanghai. A 22 year veteran of the advertising industry, he is a nine-time winner of the WPP Atticus award for original thinking in the marketing services, including three Grand Prix. His main areas of expertise lie in studying how cultures shape consumer demand, desire and branding; and low income communities. His work encompasses trend spotting and forecasting. Kunal was listed in the millennium edition of the Who's Who in the World, has spoken at leading universities including Harvard, Kellogg School of Management, Cambridge University, London Business School, Syracuse University, Peking University, Uni-versity of New South Wales and Australian National University. He is a frequent speaker at investor conferences across the world, where his deep insights into consumers in emerging markets are keenly sought. He is a prolific writer with an output that ranges from academic papers, book chapters, to columns in China International Business, Sparksheet and That's Beijing magazine. He has written three books previously, including the award-winning 'China's Creative Imperative'. His photographs have appeared in Holiday Travel India, Shots magazine; he has exhibited his photographs in Shanghai. Kunal is married to Sumona and they have two children.

AUTHOR
DAVID MAYO

David Mayo has been in Asia since 1993 and with Ogilvy & Mather since 1997. He is currently the President of Ogilvy & Mather ASEAN challenged with growth in some of the most vibrant cultures in the region. He has held a number of roles within Ogilvy including President of Ogilvy & Mather Advertising, Head of Marketing and Head of Business Development as well as several key client roles but his 'finest hour' was the founding of RedCard - one of Asia's most creatively ac-claimed Boutique Agencies - in 2001 which launched under the banner of "Commonsense and Bravery" which was the inspiration for this book. Graduating in London with a degree in Journalism and Business, David Mayo, a one-time Grave Digger, was destined for a future in London's Fleet Street until he discovered the world of Advertising. He joined Lintas London in 1985 as a Graduate Trainee. David is a member of D&AD and a Fellow of the Royal Geographical Society, he spends his own time outdoors cycling, hiking, climbing and swimming. David now lives in Singapore with his wife Jane and their three children and a menagerie of pets, bicycles and a vast collection of old signs.

*PHOTOGRAPHER
THOMAS BILLHARDT*

Thomas Billhardt's photographs are well known around the globe, having been exhibited over 100 times from Moscow to New York, as well as appearing in over 60 documentaries. His work has been published in the largest illustrated magazines, Time, Stern, Spiegel, and Paris Match. In 1961, he travelled to the revolutionary country of Cuba for the first time. This trip was to be a turning point in his life. This point of departure and the allure of the revolutionary pendulum did not leave him cold. However, he suffered the wounds that a struggle for power can inflict. His photographs testified to this fact. Thomas has travelled to just about all the crisis regions of the world in the role of photo documentarist, often putting his own life in jeopardy. He has seen and experienced more of the world than most people could cope with, from the war in Vietnam, the starving in Bangladesh, to the war in Sarajevo. His photographs relentlessly force us to see. His passion for helping the children of the war has found him working with UNICEF since 1987. Always looking for an adventure, Thomas jumped at the chance to work with his son, joining him for part of the journey through Seoul, Tokyo and Shanghai.

*PHOTOGRAPHER
STEFFEN BILLHARDT*

As the son of a famous documentary photo-grapher (Thomas Billhardt) and the grandchild of a respected portrait photographer (Maria Schmid Billhardt), Steffen was soon pulled into the circle of photography, fascinated by the thought of capturing life. While the photographs of his father played an influential role, Steffen wanted his photographs to be different. Between 1986 and 1988, he worked as a photographic reporter for a number of different publishers in Berlin. Thereafter, he studied for two years at the University of Film and Television in Potsdam, Konrad Wolf Potsdam Bebelsberg, before extending his knowledge in photography at PPS Studios Hamburg (Professional Photo Service). In 1991, he moved to the US basing himself between Miami, Florida, and NYC, and also working extensively in the Caribbean. In 2000, he made several trips to Asia and decided that this region would give him a new challenge, so in 2001 he moved to Thailand and began an on-going love affair with the region where he continues to specialize in lifestyle and fashion photography. Steffen accepted the challenge from Ogilvy to capture examples of everyday creativity in Asia, setting off on a 30 day whirlwind tour, powered by a passion for the region and supported by the local insights of Ogilvy staff in each port of call.